The Fields of David Smith

The Fields of

CANDIDA N. SMITH

With a memoir by IRVING SANDLER

Photographs by JERRY L. THOMPSON

Contributions by MARK DI SUVERO, HELEN FRANKENTHALER, ANTHONY CARO, KENNETH NOLAND, JOAN PACHNER, and others

Historical photography by DAVID SMITH, DAN BUDNIK, ALEXANDER LIBERMAN, and others

THAMES AND HUDSON

The Fields of David Smith is published in conjunction with a three-year exhibition of the same name presented at the Storm King Art Center, Mountainville, New York, in 1997, 1998, and 1999. The exhibition was organized by guest curator Candida N. Smith and Storm King director David R. Collens.

First published in Great Britain in 1999 by Thames and Hudson Ltd, London

British Library Cataloguing-in-Publication data
A catalogue record for this book is available from the British Library

ISBN 0-500-01908-8

Front cover illustration: *Untitled (Candida), 1965,* in the 1998 exhibition, with *Sentinel V,* 1959. Photograph by Jerry L. Thompson.

Back cover illustration: Detail of *XI Books III Apples,* 1959. Photograph by Jerry L. Thompson.

Half title illustration: View of the 1998 exhibition at dawn with, from left: *Personage of May,* 1957; *The Woman Bandit,* 1956–58; *XI Books III Apples,* 1959; and *Study in Arcs,* 1957. Photograph by Jerry L. Thompson.

Title page 1: South, or lower, field, Bolton Landing, in 1963, with, from left to right: 5 *Ciarcs,* 2 *Circles* 2 *Crows,* 7 *Hours,* and *Bec-Dida Day;* and *Cubis I, XI, VI,* and *VIII* (1962). All works except *Cubi VIII* from 1963. Photograph by David Smith.

Title page 2: View of the 1998 exhibition at dawn with, from left: *Construction December II,* 1964; *Primo Piano III,* 1962; *Untitled,* 1963; *Voltri VIII,* 1962; and *Portrait of a Painter,* 1954. Photograph by Jerry L. Thompson.

PRINTED AND BOUND IN ITALY

David Smith in Bill Gates's Diner, Bolton Landing, in October or November 1963. Photograph by Dan Budnik.

This book is dedicated
to the grandchildren of David Smith:
Emma, Sam, and Luke Smith-Stevens
and Hudson and Gabriel Cavanagh,
and, by marriage, Dorothy and Carroll Cavanagh III—
that they may know more of the fields in which they play
and of the spirit of the grandfather
who would have adored them.

Volton XVIII, 1963,
as installed at Bolton Landing in 1963,
with other Voltri-Boltons and Voltons.
Photograph by David Smith.

Volton XVIII, 1963,
as installed at Storm King in 1997.
Photograph by Jerry L. Thompson.

Contents

North, or upper, field, Bolton Landing in May 1965. Photograph by Alexander Liberman.

Introduction

H. PETER STERN
Chairman and President, Storm King Art Center

The sculpture of David Smith is as central to the history of Storm King Art Center as it is to the history of modern art. In 1966, the year after Smith's untimely death, Ralph E. Ogden, the founder of the Art Center, drove to see Smith's sculptures at Bolton Landing in upstate New York. He saw an amazing sight: row upon row of extraordinary abstract sculptures in the grassy fields that surrounded Smith's home and studio. The following year "Ted" Ogden and I arranged to purchase thirteen of Smith's masterworks through the Ralph E. Ogden Foundation, which donated them to the Art Center, where I was and continue to be Chairman and President.

Initially, we installed Smith's sculptures near the building in places chosen to accommodate each sculpture individually, but in 1976 we grouped them together in the newly expanded display area to the south of the museum building. We selected the new site primarily for its view of the mountains; it reminded us of Bolton Landing. Smith's sculptural presence has served as a stimulus for the Art Center's development, affecting our own evolution as profoundly as it has affected the work of the sculptors who have succeeded him.

In 1976, inspired in part by Smith's sculpture fields, our new director David R. Collens, landscape architect William A. Rutherford, Sr., and I began to reconfigure the outside viewing area, placing works outdoors so that they would be seen in relation not only to our immediate landscape, but also to one another and to the undulating profiles of the mountains of the Hudson Highlands that surround the Art Center. This new approach extended the conceptual boundaries of the Art Center far beyond its actual borders.

"The Fields of David Smith" evokes the spirit of the sculpture-filled fields that inspired Mr. Ogden more than thirty years ago. The unprecedented series of three changing exhibitions has immeasurably enriched our understanding of Smith's work and his creative process. Smith, on the evidence of his own photographs, insisted on the integral relationship of his creations with the Adirondack landscape that enveloped him at Bolton Landing. Storm King Art Center, which includes 500 acres of rolling lawns, fields, and woodlands, all ringed by the Hudson Highlands, is in a unique position to display Smith's work outdoors. We have been able, therefore, to savor the sculptures as Smith did—in relation to one another and with the ever-changing effects of light, weather, and the seasons.

This publication celebrates the three exhibitions at Storm King, which reunited sculptures that were in Smith's fields more than thirty years ago. The story is told through a combination of historical photographs taken at Bolton Landing by Dan Budnik, Alexander Liberman, Harry Gitlin, and David Smith himself, combined with new photographs by Jerry L. Thompson documenting the installations at Storm King in 1997 and 1998, and the sculptures shown in 1999. The recollections by Candida N. Smith, Irving Sandler, and Mark di Suvero make history come alive, communicating a palpable sense of what it was like to be at Bolton Landing when David Smith was working there. Further, we are pleased that our magnificent setting enables us to reflect on the larger connection between Smith's sculpture and nature.

"The Fields of David Smith" exhibitions as well as this publication result from the extraordinary collaborative effort of guest curator Candida N. Smith, our director David R. Collens, and myself. Candida N. Smith's drive and passion to expand our understanding of her late father's work merit the profound gratitude of all who have seen the three "Fields of David Smith" installations at Storm King Art Center, as well as all who enjoy this publication.

Acknowledgments *David R. Collens*

The achievement of a three-year exhibition dedicated to realizing Smith's vision for the installation and comprehension of his work has involved the generous support and efforts of many people. The moving force behind it all has been Candida N. Smith, whose knowledge of her father's work and eloquence in its explication have made both exhibition and catalogue rare visual experiences. Through a subtlety of selection and placement, Candida created a world in which Smith's art could be seen at its purest and as it was intended to be seen. Her personal engagement in helping to secure loans ensured the most evocative groupings of Smith's work year after year. We would like to add our voices to hers in saying we are especially indebted to all the lenders who parted with works that have become integrated into their lives and to the institutions whose collections and audiences rely on Smith. Nor could the exhibition or catalogue have been realized without the generous support of numerous foundations and individuals. We would also like to recognize the contribution of Rebecca Smith and Peter Stevens, Administrator of the Collection of Candida and Rebecca Smith, whose commitment, expertise, and guidance in all aspects of the exhibition have been invaluable. Adding to the acknowledgments expressed by Candida N. Smith, I want to extend my personal thanks to Rose Wood, Helen Hydos, Joyce Massowd, and Colleen Zlock of the Art Center staff for their unflagging enthusiasm and efforts, and to Jerry L. Thompson for the understanding and sensitivity to Smith's work expressed in his photography.

Acknowledgments CANDIDA N. SMITH

The extraordinary and unconventional nature of this exhibition called for equally extraordinary efforts from all the people connected with "The Fields of David Smith." My enduring gratitude, affection, and admiration go to them all. There is nothing like working with the best.

The Ralph E. Ogden Foundation, Inc., under the directorship of H. Peter Stern, has stood by and supported this exhibition and book with mountain fastness. My family and I honor them and thank them.

Peter Stern is a man of rare depth of commitment who pursued our vision unstintingly, tirelessly, and faithfully. As the scope and scale of this endeavor took on its own momentum, Peter marshaled us all to meet the challenge. I also want to thank Dr. Margaret Johns, and Lisa, Bea, and John Stern for their sustaining interest.

David R. Collens brings a deep and living love to his work with David Smith. It is a rare museum director who brings his or her utter joy to the installation of sculpture. His intimacy with the play of light and seasonal growth patterns of trees at Storm King is unique and his enthusiasm boundless. Joan Pachner, herself a Smith scholar, has been a valued member of our team, adding her erudition. I want to thank the excellent staff of Storm King Art Center and the Ralph E. Ogden Foundation, Inc., for their willingness to do what needed to be done: Georgene Zlock, Adrian Joyce, and Mary Ann Carter; Phil Cicio, Rod Parkman, Bruce Williams, and their installation and grounds crews; the docents; and George Duschele and his security staff.

Peter Stevens, Administrator of the Collection of Candida and Rebecca Smith, has worked with peerless dedication every step of the way. I greatly appreciate his invaluable advice and expertise. I can only admire, but can never hope to achieve, his patience and fortitude. I extend my warmest thanks to my sister, Rebecca Smith, for the great link our lives have forged and without whose support no project can hope to succeed. I thank my mother, Jean Freas, for her gentle support and willingness to share her memories.

My profound gratitude goes to my fellow lenders to this three-year exhibition for their sacrifices (see page 143). I salute their sense of stewardship, which inspires them to part with their important works by David Smith in support of an enhanced understanding of the artist's achievement.

The contributing photographers, each in his own way, used the lens of true affection, as well as creative comprehension, in documenting Smith's work and his process. My father was fortunate indeed to have a record of his life and work made by such artists as Dan Budnik, Harry Gitlin, Alexander Liberman, and Ugo Mulas. (Many thanks also to Mr. Liberman's assistant Crosby Coughlin for his patience and hard work.) Jerry L. Thompson rose before dawn in his tireless pursuit of sensitive portraits of sculpture at Storm King. I also want to thank Peter Stevens for supplying photographs when needed and to thank Neil Frankel for his faithful reprints of David Smith's own photography.

Sally Fisher, Barbara Flynn, and Greer Allen brought their taste and experience to this book. I thank them all for their earnest toil, perseverance, and agility in this exacting endeavor. Without each of their invaluable contributions there would be no book of worth.

My warm appreciation goes to Helen Frankenthaler, Kenneth Noland, Sir Anthony Caro, George Rickey, and Dan Budnik for sharing their memories so generously with me. They remember my father with clarity and kindness and seemed to enjoy looking back on those days. Dan in particular has put a great deal of time, effort, and affection into this exhibition and catalogue. Irving Sandler brings a unique perspective to these pages. He knew my father as a man and as an artist, and has watched the changes in art history Smith wrought. Mark di Suvero is a true friend to art and to artists, and has been consistent and generous in his support of my father's work and of this project.

The risks involved in exhibiting works of art can only be mitigated by the skill and experience of conservators and art handlers. We are extremely fortunate to work with the very best. I thank Alan Farancz and Denise Whitbeck of Farancz Conservation as well as Albert Marshall and Frederick Brown, each for a unique dedication to the preservation of David Smith's sculpture. Martina Yamin brings her special eye and delicacy to the conservation of works on paper. I thank Jamie Dearing and Bark Frameworks for exceptional support and exquisite framing. At a certain point, everything literally rests in the hands of the art movers. A miscalculation of a sculpture's balance point can bring disaster. I thank Greg Poli of Fortress F.A.E. and Graham Stewart of Art Cart and their teams for their skill, patience, and hard work.

Finally, I want to thank the other friends of the exhibition: E. A. Carmean for his brilliant work on David Smith, which first acknowledged the importance of the fields; Agnes Gund, Sam Miller, and Barnabas McHenry for their belief in the importance of this project; Luisa Kreisberg of The Kreisberg Group I thank for her passion and advocacy. My husband, Carroll Cavanagh, is my greatest support. I thank him for his faith, wisdom, and energy.

Upper field, Bolton Landing, c.1964, looking west, with, from left to right:
Cubis V and *IV*, both 1963, and *Cubi XX*, 1964; *Tower I*, 1963;
and works based on the circle: *2 Doors* and *Untitled*, 1964;
Bec-Dida Day and *Oval Node*, both *1963;*
and *Circles V*, 1963, and *I* and *II*, both 1962. Photograph by Harry Gitlin.

The Fields at Bolton Landing

The Fields of David Smith

CANDIDA N. SMITH

Bolton Landing

Our open fields on the mountaintop are fully exposed to the sky, clouds, and wind without mediation. The fields are quiet to the world but amplify the force of one's thoughts and feelings. Solitude there goes even further: the intensity of identity in that place would be more than most people could tolerate.

My father put his sculptures in our fields so that he could look at each work in relation to the natural world of the mountains and sky and also to its fellow sculptures. Again and again, he referred to his "work stream"; each work of art being as a vessel filled from the stream while never wholly separate. I understand his term to mean the flow of his identity made physically manifest—the process by which images and ideas from decades or days before inform a work in progress or yet to be made.

David Smith's fields as a place for the dialogue between sculptures evolved from his creative process, from an interplay between nature and the artist's own nature. The artist's identity makes its mark as a stream carves its channel into a mountainside.

David Smith, early in life, eschewed the clamor of New York City's art world. He outgrew its originally stimulating effects and began to feel it to be a kind of nattering that dissipated his energies. He sought a quiet, far place for the call and response to inner challenges. Supported by the power of the Adirondack Mountains and exposed to the sky, he created an environment best suited to complete concentration on his art. These mountains, once higher than the Himalayas, had been rolled and compressed by glacial action into a dense, ironlike mass. Smith's own volcanic energy could expand in this dramatic isolation. It gave him enough room to be. At the same time, the fragile subtleties of nature, such as the tracks of a fox in the snow, mirrored his own poignant delicacy.

In the world's oldest mountain range, the Adirondacks, winter is as absolute, stark, and uncompromising as my father's own character. Sound is somehow magnified in the intense cold of ten or even twenty degrees below zero. The drop of an icicle from the roof cracks in the air like a whip. In each scrunch of a boot on snow you seem to hear the cascading of crystals compressing against one another. The presence of a

David Smith at Bolton Landing, May 1965.
Photograph by Alexander Liberman.

Smith at work late in the shop,
October or November 1963.
Photograph by Dan Budnik.

In the house at Bolton Landing in July 1965: the door to the children's room at left, the door to the drawing studio (center), and the door from the living room to the patio (right). Photographs by Dan Budnik.

loyal winter bird is felt with gratitude. Fresh tracks in the snow are both an exquisite puzzle and a break in the solitude.

My father spent his last winters mostly alone, holding to a rigorous work schedule of long days in his factory-like sculpture shop, sometimes with a break or a visit with neighbors at the town diner. He worked until it became too dark and too cold in the shop to continue. He would then stop for a good dinner and some music chosen to suit his need. Afterward, he would draw or make his "sprays." He would place found objects—pieces of metal, paint can lids, even potato peelings—in place, spray paint from cans, perhaps move the objects and spray again. The results resembled the ghostings that hot metal left on the white shop floor. The sprays, done on canvas or paper, could also serve as sketches for sculptural or painterly ideas. He often worked late into the night. Solitude weighed heavily on him in those long northern winters. At such times, people are left with only their own resources. His were prodigious.

Our house was an artist's house, part of his creative process. It was built simply of cinder blocks and steel plates, with wide windows looking down on the fields falling gently away. These uncurtained "picture" windows brought the outside into the house. We lived on one floor. Below, sunk into the hillside, was space for art storage. After learning some Italian in 1962, he named a series "Primo Piano" because, he said,

In the kitchen, December 1962. Photograph by Dan Budnik.
Living room, May 1965. Photograph by Alexander Liberman.

that was where things happened in a house. It was certainly true of his dwelling. It was always full of drawings, paintings, collages, and sculptures from different periods. Around 1962, he traded some paintings for antiques; a huge sideboard, Renaissance trestle tables, and carved wooden columns that he enlivened with spray paint. He made assemblages of objects on the walls, each suited to its room. In a living room corner by the wood stove hung a Spanish spur, an arm of an Italian clock, a platter from China, a manhole cover from Brooklyn, a Greek shield—together creating a visual poem of workmanship. Tables held birds' eggs, feathers, bones, and sculpture. In the drawing studio there hung a lizard and a human head made of bread, animal skulls, a violin, a draftsman's right angle, and drawings—the constant inner voice of his work. Drawing could record ideas soaring through his mind more quickly than the labors of sculpture. The process, more gentle, more reflective, was often done late at night after dinner. I can remember waking to a living room floor covered with drying drawings. It was a little like Christmas morning; our house was transformed, touched by a magic.

In the passage to the drawing studio was the orange Dutch door to the children's room, on it an Audubon calendar, a Plaza Hotel menu, a cardboard collage spelling "Becca and Dida," and a letter from President Johnson appointing Smith to the

Smith at Bolton Landing in 1965. Photograph by Alexander Liberman.

Top: The upper field looking east, toward the house, 1965.
Detail: Thicket of sculptures against the junk pile, including *2 Doors* and *Untitled*, both 1964; *Primo Piano II*, 1962; and *Lunar Arc*, 1961. Photographs by Alexander Liberman.

Rebecca and Candida dance in dress-up.

The girls' room.
Photographs by David Smith.

President's Council on the Arts. Through the kitchen, a site of enthusiastic preparation of woodman's stew, sautéed wild mushrooms, and seven-bean chili, the door led out to the long driveway downhill. On the right was the north, or upper, field where, in the last years of his life, Smith planted dense rows of sculpture; white-painted *Circle and Box* with *Untitled*, its architectonic companion, both 1963; Voltri-Boltons; the stainless steel *Becca* (1964); the vibrantly painted *Circles I, II,* and *III,* of 1962; several massive Wagons; and, down the hill, the delicate *Lunar Arcs on 1 Leg* (1956–60) dancing by the pond. The drive then rose slightly as it passed the junk heap of elements and found objects ready for use. Arrayed against the mound on the hill, finished pieces might "cure," as he called it, over the winter into the desired state of rust. Other elements would wait until their lines and forms indicated their use to the artist.

On the other side of the drive and down by the road was the sculpture studio, known as "the shop." Outside, finished pieces and works in progress clustered against the walls. Inside was a fully equipped metal shop with, among other tools, acetylene and arc welders, hoists, cutters, and grinders. David Smith would work on several different pieces at one time, perhaps a Cubi, a Voltri-Bolton, a Primo Piano and an Albany. He hung metal fragments and found objects against the white wall, echoing the white painted rectangles on the floor against which he would arrange pieces of steel into a sculpture.

From one end of the shop an open deck extended into space as the ground beneath it fell sharply down to a pond. To the left, the upper field climbed toward the house, while the lower field swept down in its profile. A patio encircled the house, most generously on the side facing the sloping south, or lower, field. On the margin of this patio ring, small sculptures from different periods were mounted on pedestals of stacked cinder block, marble, or slate. Larger pieces, those with the mass of a seated human, such as *Personage from Stove City* (1946) and *Blue Construction* (1938), were placed inside the ring. Below the terrace, just beyond the small flower garden, there sometimes stood larger, human-scale pieces. Finally, stretching across two fields, were the largest monumental sculptures, arranged and rearranged to suit Smith's meditative needs. These were not at all "curated" in the traditional sense of being consciously ordered so as to explain themselves, but rather disposed to challenge each other and provoke discourse of imagery, volume, space, and line. They were Sentinels, Totems, Gates, Zigs, Wagons, Circles, and Towers, just as Smith called them. I felt them also to be witnesses, warriors, companions, and places for exploration.

Smith often said he made only girl sculptures. He explained:

> I don't make boy sculptures. They become kind of personages, and sometimes they cry out to me that I should have been better or bigger, and mostly they tell me that I should have done that twelve years before—or twenty years before.[1]

To me, the voices of many of the Voltri-Boltons challenge "who goes there?" with a weapon to hand. Human scale, they confront the viewer with that most probing of questions. *Three Ovals Soar* (1960) reaches to lyric heights with a beauty that squeezes the human heart. *Rebecca Circle* (1961) bursts with an epigrammatic wit, then flashes its other face of a totemic wildflower. The Cubi "gates" are open portals designating a picture plane of imbued space waiting for us to enter and be transformed. The Sentinels stand eternally watching. They do not bar our way; they stand witness for the everlasting record, reflecting our movement back to us in their stainless surfaces. *Superstructure on 4* (1960) stands on stilts to reflect only sky and clouds.

My own relationship to these sculptures was casual, intimate, and profound, as was appropriate to siblings who share a progenitor. My sister and I often played in the lower field. We picked berries, and at night watched for shooting stars and told ghost stories. We made banging music with our fists on steel. In winter we attempted sledding, which was always difficult because of the deep snow and large sculptures. In summer we fished in the pond at the bottom of the upper field, casting into the reflections of the willow elm, *Windtotem* (1962), or *Study in Arcs* (1957). To children a pond is a water world for rowing, frog catching, and mud treading. Comforting, homey sounds of the grinder or welding torch came from the nearby shop, telling us that our father or Leon Pratt, his assistant, were always close enough to come over to get the hook out of the mouth of an unfortunate perch.

In later years of growing up, after my father's death, the fields were a good place to

Above: Materials in the sculpture shop, 1965. Photograph by Alexander Liberman.

Smith finishing *Tower 1*, March 1963. Photograph by Dan Budnik.

Smith making *Voltri-Bolton X*, 1962.
Photographs by Dan Budnik.

look for the answers and apparitions adolescents demand so stridently. The ground there felt to me to be the most solid, heavily imbued part of my world.

The Great Quiet of Stopped Machines

Before the turn of the twentieth century, when much of the Adirondack area was cut for timber, the fields at Bolton Landing were cleared. The region was never a successful one for agriculture. The land is steep, the soil acidic, and the ground pushes up rocks at a rate to break a farmer's heart. Still, there are remains of elegant nineteenth-century dry walls, held together by skill and gravity, marking two sides of the south field. In the late 1920s, when Smith first visited and then purchased the property, it was a fox farm. All that is documented of Smith's use of the fields in the early years—the 1930s and 1940s—is that Smith and Dorothy Dehner, then his wife, planted a small fruit orchard near the house. On the evidence of a single photograph (page 37), we know that painted wooden constructions were set into the upper field.

So many of David Smith's ideas were part of his vision from the beginning. The vision of his sculpture in nature seems always to have been there. Throughout his career in sculpture, from the early days on a Brooklyn wharf, working in the original Terminal Iron Works, Smith would photograph his sculpture outdoors.

In the Adirondacks he consistently made photographic portraits of works outside, often on the Bolton Landing town dock or on one of its pylons, measuring the piece against the lake and mountains. Eye level was often low, enhancing a sense of monumentality. He also went to enormous physical effort in the later years to arrange large pieces temporarily for photography before they went out for exhibition.

In the late 1940s and through the 1950s the patio overlooking the south field was often dense with sculpture. *Star Cage* (1950) and *Blackburn, Song of an Irish Blacksmith* (1949–50) were among them. A few pieces, including *The Fish* (1950), took up a temporary residence in the field beyond. According to my mother, Jean Freas, Smith's second wife, *Australia* (1951) was the first to be placed squarely in the center of the field beyond the house. David Smith was well aware that *Australia,* with its fluid gestures of a long arm swinging gracefully, was an extremely important piece, heralding a new era for his work. It represented a culmination of his sinuous use of metal and the technique of drawing in space. Thus planted, *Australia* drew not just in any space—such as the impartial space of a museum gallery—but in the specific landscape of Bolton Landing. The fields were truly born.

The sculptures grew larger and more numerous as money for materials trickled in

Portrait of a Painter, 1954, and *The Sitting Printer,* 1954-55,
photographed on the town dock at Bolton Landing, Lake George in the background.
Photograph by David Smith.

more regularly through the 1950s. Each sculpture was carefully sited and mounted on a sunken cast-cement pedestal. The 1960s rapidly brought increased critical acclaim and more financial rewards. More materials meant more and larger pieces. David Smith had more energy and creative ideas than he could handle.

The spring of 1962 brought Smith to Italy as a participant in the fourth Festival of Two Worlds, in Spoleto. He was given a team of workers, his choice of the area's abandoned factories, and all the metal pieces he could salvage in return for the creation of one sculpture to be displayed in Genoa. In a phenomenal explosion of artistic output, he made twenty-seven sculptures in thirty days. This was larger than the sum of all the other sculptural work in the festival put together. Giovanni Carandente, the festival's director, installed the entire series, called Voltri after the town of their fabrication, in Spoleto's ancient Roman amphitheater.

My father's excited anticipation can literally be read in his sculpture. The only time he ever wrote words with the grinder was when he scrawled on the side of *Voltri VI*, "Voltri Andanno Spoleto."

In his notes "Report on Voltri" he wrote about "finding" elements for sculpture as a process of recognition in "the great quiet of stopped machines—the awe, the pull. . . . Part is personal heritage. . . . Since I've had identity, the desire to create excels over the desire to visit [the ancient sites and museums]."

> The beauties of the forge shop, parts dropped partly forged, cooled now but stopped in progress—as if the human factor had dissolved and the great dust settled—the found tombs of early twentieth century, from giants to tweezers headed for the open hearth to feed the world's speediest rolls. Archaeologists have their iron interests back 5,000 years. In the yard where iron has lain shedding scale and scrap, punchings scraps from shearing, I found parts of my nature not over seventy years old in the first inch, but this flat beside a stream near the sea may, farther down, hold museum iron. I brought back to Bolton handfuls of findings for no greater reason than that they fit with my miscellany and complement the manhole cover from Brooklyn which hangs on my wall.
>
> The archaeologists may go as far as L.S.B. Leakey and fill many halls, but my vision is in dreaming the host of events destroyed in their time. It is possible the museums are too small in truth to form historianisms.[2]

It should be noted that his "handfuls" were more like truckloads.

My father returned home that summer invigorated and jubilant. I had never seen him quite so happy. Before that summer, there were a few sculptures around the pond at the bottom of the upper field. It was after his return from Italy that the fields began

Smith working in an abandoned factory in Voltri, 1962.
Photograph by Ugo Mulas, courtesy of Antonia, Valentina, and Melina Mulas, Milan.

to burgeon at an amazing rate. It was as if the creative explosion and the resulting enormous installation in Spoleto ignited a fire that did not burn out. The Voltri-Boltons were made along with the painted circle pieces, Primo Pianos, Zigs, and Cubis. The upper fields that had been nearly empty before the summer of '62 filled with increasing density throughout the last three years of his life.

Looking at large groups of his own work gave him a peaceful sense of release—parts of his nature were realized and therefore taken care of. There was also the exhilaration of accomplishment. He came home to Bolton Landing with tremendous momentum and set to work to fill the fields of his "sculpture farm."

Using the Fields

In the years I knew my father, we used the fields around our house fully and constantly. Each morning began with a long look out the window toward the lower field that slid away from the house down to the woods below, then to the wedge of lake, mysterious at this distance, but intimately familiar through our memories of plunking in its water. The eye then reached out to far-away mountaintops stretching into Vermont. Often in the morning, clouds would settle into little valleys between the ridges, their tops rising like dragons among the trees. These "dragons" or the sightings of a visiting fox family strangely mottled orange and silver—descendants of the silver foxes raised earlier on our property—gave us the first real news of the day.

> How little I know—until I see what happened in the night on the snow—
> the movement of animals, their paths, and why—the animals
> that fly the night birds leave no tracks except on the mind
> the star tracks that angle to the earth sharp and direct
> the broad brushing of the wind shown only by the snow plops
> from branches—circuling the bushes and trees.[3]

Observation was an honored skill in my father's house.

Mornings, he would walk to the edge of the terrace and let out a huge roar, I imagine to release feelings built up overnight and announce his return to the waking world.

In summer, we often ate breakfast in our pajamas on the terrace looking out on the possibilities of the day. My father encouraged my sister and me to run among the sculptures, to climb, to put our bodies into the elements of the sculptures, to bang out tuneless rhythms and hear the difference between the sound of flat and volumetric elements. It was a playground for the unconscious. One summer my father built a house of straw and one of twigs and set up an army tent in the upper field for our play, when we weren't playing pirate in a rowboat in the pond at the bottom of the field.

The lower field in 1963 with Cubis and related stainless steel works, from left: *Cubi XII*, 1963; *Three Circles and Planes*, 1959; *8 Planes 7 Bars*, .1957-58; *March Sentinel*, 1961; *Sentinel V*, 1959; *Superstructure on 4*, 1960; *Cubi III*, 1961, and *Cubi I*, 1963. Photograph by David Smith.

"The Birthday": dancing to the band and eating cupcakes. Photographs by David Smith and an unknown photographer.

Each summer at this time brought what he called "The Birthday." We were rarely together for my sister's April birthday so we celebrated both of our birthdays together in August. It was a huge party with friends from New York, Provincetown, Vermont, and a large area around Bolton Landing. David Smith made a five-foot lollipop tree, spray-painted and drilled with holes into which the sticked candies were inserted so that the construction bristled. We had an M&M's stand with piles of the treasure to give away. A magic bird, mounted on a tall stand, was spray-painted pink and gold and had a long plumed tail made of sequined organza to blow in the breeze.

Children and their mamas, dressed in their party best, danced on the terrace to the music of the combo from the town's good hotel. Wine and ginger ale flowed freely, and mountainous marvels of ice cream were passed around in soda fountain bowls. I don't remember any cake, but we were big on ice cream. Balloons and streamers fluttered from trees by the house, and spray-painted golf balls and a bright buoy hung from certain trees like fantastical fruit. We always had pony or donkey rides, the animal borrowed from a neighbor. One year the pony ran away to the bottom of the field with our favorite neighbor child. She was rescued in tears and the rides ended, but we all posed for photos with the forgiven offender. One year we fired a salute from a Revolutionary-era cannon dredged from a local pond. Our well always went dry by the end of the day, depleted by unknowing city folks. We never cared.

Rebecca and Candida with *Australia.* Photographs by David Smith.

"The Birthday" is the subject of *Bec-Dida Day* (1963)—a splendid celebration exploding out of time—complete unto itself. This sculpture my father set in the same field where the party took place. Our play was part of the fields as much as were the sculptures, for Smith as well as for his daughters. He needed to hold these simple satisfactions—fun, and well-fed girls—in his other times of loneliness and in the sometimes violent turmoil of his emotional life.

I believe that gazing out at his fields, as he so often did, he found a kind of peace in the balance of the sculptures, which were like so many aspects of his identity. Physically manifested and set out together to form their own dialogue—ultimately aesthetic—the sculptures in the fields brought a kind of musical order to the dissonance of his inner flow of feeling. He always said that for him, art was easier to do than life.

The Battle of Being

Art is made from dreams, and visions, and things not known, and least of all from things that can be said. It comes from the inside of who you are when you face yourself. It is an inner declaration of purpose, it is a factor which determines artist identity. . . .

I will not change an error if it feels right, for the error is more human than perfection. I do not seek answers. I haven't named this work nor thought where it would go. I haven't thought what it is for, except that it is made to be seen. I've made it because it comes closer to saying who I am than any other method I can use. This work is my identity. There were no words in my mind during its creation, and I'm certain words are not needed in its seeing; and why should you expect understanding when I do not? That is the marvel—to question but not to understand. Seeing is the true language of perception. Understanding is for words. As far as I am concerned, after I've made the work, I've said everything I can say.[4]

For David Smith, his identity as an artist was the personal foundation of everything he did and was. It was as clear to him as the tablets to Moses. It was the dearly won prize from long years of struggle in the "battle of being," as he called it. From that core of identity he could consistently strike with utter conviction with the brush on paper, the alignment of sculptural elements on the shop floor, or any other medium, and the stroke would be guided inevitably by that inner compass. Identity is the sum total of personal truth, and conviction is the force with which identity is expressed. There was no intermediary, as he always said; his art was his identity.

My father acted at all times and in all aspects of his life from his identity as an artist. He had no other. He cooked with the extravagant generosity and adventurousness of an artist. He parented as an artist—his children should not wear "pretty" colors, but rather "gutsy" colors. Our imaginations should not be constrained by mass-market toys. He could devour music. If dirty dishes became too demanding in winter, he stuck them in the snow to wait for spring thaw. He saw himself as outside of and in opposition to the class-structured society.

While he could be generous, spontaneous, playful, and hospitable, his sense of "I am" was all about "I am an artist." There was little room to identify himself in terms of other people. And so he felt lonesome.

My father never knew what a work block was. Ideas rushed in much too fast for him to realize them all. Some remained in the form of spray drawings or notebook sketches. Any problems that did not resolve themselves through the labor of sculpture making could be drawn or painted through.

I maintain my identity by regular work, there is always labor when inspiration

Constructions in the upper field, c. 1932.
Photograph by David Smith.

Lower field looking north toward the house,
with *Circle IV,* 1962, in the foreground,
and visible in the middle ground, from left to right:
7 Hours, 1963; *Sentinel V,* 1959; *Superstructure on 4,* 1960;
Fifteen Planes, 1958; *Cubi III,* 1961; *XI Books and III Apples,* 1959;
and *Three Circles and Planes,* 1959. Photograph by Dan Budnik.

has fled, but inspiration returns quicker when identity and the work stream are maintained. [5]

Courage kept him going. With it he created and lived his identity as an artist with absolute fidelity. When his work was not appreciated, understood, or financially supported, he knew his achievements better than anyone else. He would listen with interest to those he respected. Then he would do exactly as he saw fit. Discouragement—that is, to be distanced from his courage—was a personal form of hell, excruciating but short-lived.

My father said that he did not judge one piece against another. This was also true of aspects of his identity. Most people learn to hide or disguise the darker parts of their unconscious; he had learned to keep them right in front of him in the air and light of the mountaintop. He listened carefully to his demons, dreams, and visions; they guided him well. With them he recognized aspects of his nature in found objects. His strokes when broadest became geometric and abstract. Still, the conviction behind them struck with a force of honesty and authenticity as to be utterly human. Any diminution of absolute integrity was dangerous to his mind.

The direct experience of art, unpolluted by academia or the marketplace, was the manner of his life. In the landscape he created a multilevel discourse, complete and unedited. There was the dialogue between the works, and another between nature and the artist's nature. Many totemic works, especially the Sentinels and certain Cubis, are about the artist's stance in the world—tall, heroic, and solitary. The sculpture acts upon the landscape, transforming it as an endowed, highly charged arena just as a dance defines the space of its performance. Particular works also reinterpret the space of nature. The white *Oval Node* (1963), for example, or *Lunar Arc* (1961) seems to "punch out" part of nature, continuing the negative-positive spatial exchange of the spray drawings and the white shop floor with the darker singed ghostings left by hot metal. The Newark Museum's *Untitled* (1964) circle and other open Circle pieces seem to "target" those chunks of landscape seen through the open centers. Ambient colors are reflected from the burnished stainless steel. Shapes and colors that are found in the natural world, but on a radically new scale, as in *Rebecca Circle* (1961), refer to a wildflower or, in *2 Circles 2 Crows* (1963), to the shapes of birds flying overhead.

Thus the great discourse of David Smith's sculpture fields is framed by mountainous space. It was a magnificent creation, ever evolving, ever changing, each sculpture independently a great work of art, together a radical congress of aesthetic discourse poignant in its humanness.

December 1963.
Photograph
by Dan Budnik.

When I saw that David places his work against the mountains and sky,
the impulse was plain, an ineffable desire to see his humanness related to exterior reality,
to nature at least if not man, for the marvel of the felt scale that exists
between a true work and the immovable world, the relation that makes both human.

— ROBERT MOTHERWELL
Art in America, January–February 1966, p. 37

NOTES

1 David Smith, *David Smith by David Smith,* edited by Cleve Gray (New York: Thames and Hudson, 1968), p. 87.
2 David Smith, "Report on Voltri," in *David Smith,* edited by Garnett McCoy (New York: Praeger, 1973), p. 158.
3 Smith, *David Smith by David Smith,* p. 144. As a passionate admirer of James Joyce, Smith sometimes invented his own words. "Circuling" may be a combination of of "circling" and "culling."
4 Smith, "Tradition and Identity,"in *David Smith,* pp. 147–48. Speech given at Ohio University, Athens, Ohio, April 17, 1959.
5 Smith, "Notes for 'David Smith Makes a Sculpture,'" published by Elaine de Kooning in *ARTnews,* January 1969. In *David Smith,* p. 77.

The David Smith I Knew

MARK DI SUVERO

David Smith had the heavy animal energy of an industrial worker, the capacity, the craftsmanship and the will of an original artist, and he drank his booze (whiskey) in a way that made me shudder. He was a modernist, an abstract sculptor who, like most American artists of the mid-twentieth century, was deeply impressed by European Cubism and found his psychological reflection in his sculpture.

His development was American-quirky, and he tried to bring the methods and means of industrial society's factory to the level of high art. He succeeded more than he knew, for they called him the Dean of American welded sculpture. But aside from one issue of *Arts Magazine*, U.S. art criticism treated him condescendingly, and he had little financial success in his lifetime (unlike Pollock and de Kooning).

He wanted to be an action painter, and the magnificent swirling grind-patterns on stainless steel can only be done by a wild bull of a man. But steel takes care and craftsmanship, and spatial sculpture takes thought—the slow intensity of welding. He was a master.

I met David at a group show at the Jewish Museum. He gave me one of those great compliments that enhearten a young artist for a whole lifetime. It came out of an inclusive generosity of his spirit toward other artists and was so unlike the petty jockeying of cynical artists.

I went to see him at Bolton Landing (with John Chamberlain, Henry Geldzahler, and John Hopkins) to ask him how to cut stainless steel. He showed me by cutting a four-inch stainless strap with a flexible-shaft friction wheel, with no ear protection. SCREAM! They hadn't invented the plasma arc.

I was so impressed by his field of sculpture that I wrote him a poem for Becca and Dida, which he remembered and mentioned the last time I saw him, at his show at Marlborough-Gerson. He was the first artist that I met who used a bridge crane, and the young sculptors of my generation were in awe of him. His recognition of factory forms as sculptures (the Voltris) and his use of open space (*Star Cage, Australia, Hudson River Landscape*) made him the most influential sculptor (*Five Units Equal* was the first minimalist sculpture) of his generation. He was a great American sculptor.

Photograph by Alexander Liberman, 1965.

David Smith, A Memoir

IRVING SANDLER

The installation of David Smith's welded constructions in the fields of Storm King in the Hudson Highlands recalls the way he positioned them in his Bolton Landing "sculpture farm," as he called it, in the Adirondacks. Indeed, the landscape of up-state New York is their natural habitat. David told art critic Thomas Hess that he designed many of his constructions for outdoors and preferred stainless steel because it was the most practical material. "I polished [the sculptures] in such a way that on a dull day, they take on the dull blue, or the color of the sky in the afternoon sun, the glow, golden like the rays, the colors of nature. . . . They are colored by the sky and surroundings, the green or blue of water."[1]

I visited David in Bolton Landing in the summer of 1964, but I first met him in 1955 at the Cedar Tavern, the favorite hangout of the Abstract Expressionists, and we continued to see each other on and off until his death. As was my practice I jotted down what he said—in longhand since this was the pre-tape-recorder era. Much of this brief memoir is based on those notes.

David spoke of growing up in Indiana and Ohio—without art. Inadvertently, however, a few of his boyhood and teenage activities did contribute to his later art making. Son of a telephone company technician and part-time inventor, he tinkered with telephones, taking them apart and playing with their innards. He also collected junk, which he sold for pocket money, anticipating his later incorporation of found metal into his constructions. David revealed an artistic inclination as early as high school. He became the school cartoonist and drew the illustrations for the school yearbook. He also took a correspondence course in cartooning from a Cleveland art school.

David came to New York City in 1926 at age nineteen and soon encountered the modern arts. Even some three decades later, when he recalled it, he conveyed the excitement of attending a production of Stravinsky's *The Firebird* and seeing Cubist paintings and collages. He also read James Joyce's novels—for the first of many times. David was open to new art and ideas then and would remain open all of his life. He said to Thomas Hess: "I love things I . . . don't know about. I don't understand why other people don't."[2]

David enrolled at the Art Students League soon after arriving in New York. From 1927 to 1931, he studied painting with Jan Matulka, as did his wife Dorothy Dehner, as well as Burgoyne Diller, Edgar Levy, and George McNeil. Matulka taught them

The upper field of Bolton Landing in winter 1967. Photograph by Dan Budnik.

about Cubist picture making and also introduced them to Constructivism and the nonobjective painting of Mondrian and Kandinsky. David said that after listening to Matulka one could never take abstract art lightly. Above all, David was inspired by his mentor's independence and courage since he sensed that Matulka's teaching, which was strongly opposed by his hidebound colleagues, would probably lead to his dismissal from the League. It did, although the reason given was that his class was underenrolled.

David gravitated to avant-garde artists and became friendly with Stuart Davis, John Graham, Arshile Gorky, Willem de Kooning, Jean Xceron, and Mischa Resnikoff. They formed a loose group, meeting informally at various Greenwich Village hangouts—Romany Marie's Restaurant, Stewart's Cafeteria, McSorley's Tavern. De Kooning recalled, "We didn't talk about personalities—only art. We were all poor and worried only about the work. It [was] all artistic ideas."[3] David said that he felt like a student, but they treated him as an equal. He added that he was lucky to have been accepted into this circle. In his influential book, *System and Dialectics of Art,* Graham hailed David, along with Milton Avery, Stuart Davis, and Willem de Kooning, among others, as "young outstanding American painters."[4] He wrote that in 1936—that early—even before David's first solo show two years later. Subsequently, Graham would say, "David was the best sculptor in America."[5]

Picasso was the artist David and his friends admired most, Graham calling him the greatest artist past, present—and, most likely, future. But they experimented with every other style. De Kooning recalled:

> There was a terrific amount of activity going on in the thirties. It was not a dead period. You don't have to like the art to appreciate the excitement. But many of the people were good artists—Graham, Davis, Gorky. We knew one another. But we also respected American Scene and Social Realist artists. Gorky and Soyer were good friends. I wasn't a member of the American Abstract Artists, but I was with them. I disagreed with their narrowness, their telling me not to do something. We fooled around with all kinds of things and changed from style to style a lot. It was a great big hodge-podge.[6]

It is noteworthy that in 1938 David joined the American Abstract Artists—most of whose members were programatically nonobjective—and exhibited abstract sculptures in their shows, while at the same time he was modeling his figurative Medals for Dishonor.

After he was dismissed from the Art Students League, Matulka became something of a recluse. He continued to paint but not to exhibit. David maintained contact with his former teacher and tried to have his paintings shown. He urged Clement Greenberg and me to see them, and once in the late 1950s he shepherded us personally to Matulka's apartment. We viewed the paintings in his living room. Lacking space, Matulka had tacked multiple canvases onto stretchers and flipped them like fabric samples. His work had not diverged much from the Synthetic Cubism he had been painting while at the League, but it remained very accomplished. Greenberg and I were impressed with what we saw but could not think of a gallery to suggest.

I was touched repeatedly by David's generosity. For example, in 1959, long after his separation and divorce from Dorothy Dehner, he mailed me two photographs of her work and an announcement of her show at the Willard Gallery, urging me not to miss it. In his covering letter he wrote, "She has her own nature."[7]

David got the latest news about art in Paris from Graham, who made frequent trips there, and, like most modernist artists in New York, by reading *Cahiers d'art*, though, in David's case, by looking at the reproductions, since he didn't know French. (Artists generally went to the New York Public Library to read art magazines because they couldn't afford to buy them and because the library was heated, unlike their cold-water studios.) David began to think of moving from painting to sculpture after he saw illustrations of Picasso's constructions in space in *Cahiers d'art* in 1929. It occurred to him then that iron construction could be his forte. He had worked on the assembly line at the Studebaker automobile plant in South Bend, Indiana, and in general was familiar with metal work. *Cahiers d'art* also published illustrations of Lipchitz's "transparencies" in 1930 and 1932; Giacometti's *Palace at Three A.M.* and other sculptures in 1932; Pablo Gargallo's forged sculptures in 1934 (they had been exhibited at New York's Brummer Gallery, in a show David had seen); and González's iron constructions in 1933 and 1934. David did not pay much attention to González until Graham gave him one of his sculptures in 1934, but his appreciation grew, especially when in 1956 he wrote an article on him in *ARTnews* entitled "González, First Master of the Torch."[8]

David was immersed in modernist art. He often spoke of his passion for Cubism, although he once said (with a smile) that he might still have arrived at his construction sculpture if he had never encountered Picasso's collages and constructions, since he had read James Joyce's *Ulysses*; his "verbal knowing" would have sufficed. David also schooled himself in Surrealism, which he learned about from *Cahiers d'art* and other magazines, such as *Transition* and *This Quarter*, whose Surrealist number of September 1932 he never forgot.

At times David's sculpture expressed his social consciousness, as in the Medals for Dishonor, which derided munition making, gas and germ warfare, aerial bombardment, and other social outrages. He also viewed his welded construction in broader social terms, maintaining that iron and steel were *the* modernist sculptural mediums.

"The metal itself possesses little art history. What associations it possesses are those of this century: power, structure, movement, progress, suspension, destruction, brutality."[9]

I once asked David whether many of his pieces verged on two-dimensionality because he had been a painter. He said that this was true perhaps in his use of color, but that he did not think about flatness and frontality. "I made my constructions like drawings. If you could draw on paper, you could make it with steel rods. A construction was a drawn object you could pick up. I reject all definitions of painting and sculpture." David then turned the conversation to music. He said that single instrumental pieces resembled line drawings, and he particularly liked unaccompanied cello and clarinet pieces.

Direct welding was vital to David. I was the art critic for the *New York Post* in the early 1960s and once ran into him on my rounds. He asked if I was going to review the bronze casts of Julio González's iron constructions then on view. Before I could answer, he urged me not to because they denied the direct process of welding.

David did not confine himself to sculpture. Indeed, his body of work is distinguished by its variety. One series that ran into the hundreds consisted of spatter pictures. He would place pieces of paper and/or objects onto papers painted white and spray the surfaces with industrial pigments. Once the papers and/or objects were removed, the white images that emerged looked like the ghosts of his constructions.

In 1959 he exhibited these pictures at the French and Company Gallery. I covered the show for *ARTnews* and wrote a review acclaiming the work. I met David soon after the review appeared, and he thanked me for it, remarking that it was the only wholeheartedly favorable one that the show received. I said that I liked the pictures so much I would like to buy one—paying for it in installments, of course. He said, "I ought to give you one, but I won't. I'm a professional artist. Do you have five dollars?" I said I did. He said: "It's five dollars down and five on delivery."

In August 1964 my wife, Lucy, and I visited David in Bolton Landing to collect our picture. He took us for a tour of the fully equipped factory that he had built there—he had named it the Terminal Iron Works—and the bucolic landscape with its idyllic views of woods, meadows, hills, and lake, in which the workshop was set. He had installed some six dozen large pieces outdoors that stood like sentinels, a title he would use for a number of constructions he began in 1956. I was struck by how well the works fit into their natural surround, how they mutually enhanced one another. It also became clear to me how much the Bolton Landing environment influenced David's sculpture. Although his fabrication was machine-shop, his subject matter was rarely machine-age, despite his use of iron and steel. His images generally referred to the human figure and the natural world. Smith himself recognized the connection

Smith cutting out a circle from sheet steel for *Primo Piano III*, December 1962. Photograph by Dan Budnik.

Smith relaxing with visitors,
including Helen Frankenthaler,
Alexander Liberman,
and Robert Motherwell
in the living room, 1965.
Photograph by Alexander Liberman.

Smith working on cardboard studies for *Cubis IV* and *V*, 1962.

Sorting through objects in the junk pile, 1962. Photographs by Dan Budnik.

between his work, visual reality, and his life. As he told David Sylvester: "My sculpture is part of my world; it's part of my everyday living; it reflects my studio, my house, my trees, the nature of the world I live in."[10]

A number of pieces outdoors were painted either in color or in white. As David said to Hess: "I've been painting sculpture all my life. . . . Painting and sculpture both, beats either one. . . . Sometimes you deny the structure of steel. And sometimes you make it appear with all its force in whatever shape it is. No rules."[11] He pointed to an all-white piece and remarked that he had put seventeen coats of white on it before he got the color right. In my 1959 review of his spray pictures I had noted that the white images resembled his constructions. I also related the spattered backgrounds to the unspoiled Lake George settings against which he liked to place his sculptures.[12] In the actual landscape, I saw clearly how closely connected the pictures and the welded constructions were.

David's studio-factory was crowded with sculpture in progress. But such was his productivity that there was work everywhere in the house as well. One room was filled with drawings, both abstract and figurative; another, with ceramic plates; and still another with spattered pictures. While looking through some of his drawings with us, David commented that as a professional artist he tried to complete one drawing a day, no matter what. He put Lucy and me in the room of spattered pictures—they were on tables and in drawers—told us to choose one, and left. We selected about a dozen and were trying to make our final choice when David returned. Studying his work with us, he asked if we didn't mind his holding out two or three. He said that he could use them as "seed" for sculpture.

At one point while we were in the fields looking at his work, we saw a huge earthmover wending its way up the mountain toward David's place. We walked to the gate to meet it. A town foreman greeted David and told him that a metal part had broken and would he please fix it. David asked whether he had the forms authorizing payment for his labor. The foreman shrugged and said dejectedly that he would have to write them up in triplicate and present them for approval to the town authorities. They both looked at each other for a prolonged moment, and the foreman said, "Okay, David, what do you want?"

"A shed right there." He pointed to where materials had been laid out.

"Okay, boys, give him his shed."

I was touched by the familiarity and fondness in their bantering. David felt very much a part of the Lake George community. He took us to dinner in a local Italian restaurant. As we entered he was greeted by name by his fellow townspeople. His delight and pride in that recognition showed, just as it had, it occurred to me, in Courbet's

View of the upper field in spring 1965. From foreground back into space: : *Cubi I*, 1963; *Untitled (Candida)*, 1965; *Wagon I*, 1964; *Primo Piano II*, 1962; and *2 Circle IV*, 1962; with *Circles V, I, II,* and *III*, 1962–63, visible in the middle ground. Photograph by Alexander Liberman.

painting, *Bonjour, Monsieur Courbet*. The Lake George area was more than a place in which to live and work. It was a place to identify with. The people there had become his people. David's community encompassed both metropolitan and rural America.

Did David's work reveal his American roots? Perhaps in his tinkering and choice of machine-shop fabrication. He was a modernist, intent on making new art. Was there any relationship between his American identity and modernism? The eighteenth-century traveler Crèvecoeur (writing as Hector St. John) defined the American as "a new man who acts on new principles; he must therefore entertain new ideas and form new opinions."[13] David's decision to locate his factory-studio in the pastoral Adirondack Mountains has a peculiarly American dimension. It was as if he tried to reconcile the two antithetical visions that Leo Marx defined in his book *The Machine in the Garden*: on the one hand, the idealized belief in America as a New Eden in which its inhabitants would lead a simpler life, closer to nature, as evoked in the writings of Cooper, Thoreau, Melville, Frost, and Hemingway; on the other hand, the regard for industrial might, which has had an equally powerful hold on the American consciousness.

Much as David and I were friends, I sensed that he was suspicious of my role as art critic. Once sitting together in Bradley's Bar, in response to a comment he made, I said, "But David, that doesn't make sense." He responded, smiling, "What can a critic know?"

Later, looking over his 1954 notebook in the Archives of American Art, I came across the following jotted down in longhand. "The secret . . . inner identity [of the artist] is seldom talked about and should be always secret. Words lead us into cliches not involved with the order of art-making or the visions which are the artist's references. Art comes from dreams and visions and not [from] verbal philosophies."[14]

NOTES

1 Thomas B. Hess, "An Interview with David Smith, June 1964 (New York: Marlborough-Gerson Gallery, October 1964), n.p.
2 Hess, "An Interview."
3 Irving Sandler, "Conversations with de Kooning," *Art Journal*, Fall 1989, p. 217.
4 Marcia Epstein Allentuck, *John Graham's System and Dialectics of Art* (Baltimore: Johns Hopkins Press, 1971), p. 154. Graham's book was fist published in 1937.
5 Dorothy Dehner, foreword to Allentuck, *John Graham's System*, p. xiv.
6 Sandler, "Conversations with de Kooning," p. 217.
7 David Smith, letter to Irving Sandler, January 26, 1959.
8 David Smith, "González: First Master of the Torch," *ARTnews*, February 1956, pp. 35–37, 64–65. Among the things that David learned about González only after he had seen his sculpture were the facts that González had constructed Picasso's metal sculptures in the late 1920s and that he had taught Gargallo how to work with iron. See also David Smith, "Notes on My Work," *Arts*, February 1960, p. 44.
9 David Smith, "The New Sculpture," in *David Smith*, edited by Garnett McCoy (New York: Praeger, 1973), p. 84. Paper given at a symposium on "The New Sculpture" at the Museum of Modern Art, February 21, 1952.
10 David Sylvester, "David Smith: Interviewed by David Sylvester," *Living Arts 3*, April 1964, p. 5.
11 Hess, "An Interview."
12 I[rving]. H. S[andler]., "Reviews and Previews: David Smith," *ARTnews*, September 1959, p. 9.
13 Quoted in Harold Rosenberg, *Tradition of the New* (New York: Horizon Press, 1959), p. 13.
14 The David Smith Papers, Archives of American Art, Smithsonian Institution.

Smith with *Cubis IV* and *V*, 1963. Photograph by Dan Budnik.

Dave would measure the sculpture against nature.
He wanted to see how well the paint held up with weather;
would it fade, chip off, and so on.
When he did something, he did it absolutely.
He meant for it to stand up to anything: nature, aesthetics, anything.
When you work in isolation
it only takes a few people around to confirm what you are doing.
The ones that came up got the message. It was pretty impressive.
David had built a kind of museum.

—KENNETH NOLAND

Smith with Voltri-Boltons, Voltons, and V.B.s outside the shop in 1963.
Photograph by Dan Budnik.

I think the sculptures kept David company, because he was lonely up there.
I think he just loved to look at them.
I used to say, "Henry Moore puts all his sculptures out in his fields
because he wants to tell the whole world that he's the greatest.
But I think David Smith puts his sculptures out in the field
to tell himself he's the greatest."
It was true in a way, because he wasn't half as confident as he seemed.
He knew he was good, but he wasn't getting a lot of praise at the time, from the world.

— ANTHONY CARO

Stainless Window, 1951. Stainless steel, 34¾" × 28¼" × 7⅞" (88.27 × 71.76 × 20 cm).
The Menil Collection, Houston. Gift of Solomon Byron Smith and Barbara Neff Smith.
Photograph by David Smith.

The terrace in winter 1963 with a view of the lower field. Photograph by Dan Budnik.

He was a wonderful host, a great host.
A ribald and beautiful human being, with a roar of laughter.
And as troubled and pained and tormented as he was,
he was large and funny. And he had a great taste for the elegance in life,
along with the crudeness.
He would get a silk shirt and sit in a three-star New York restaurant,
and he was really there.
And he'd be telling the tale of a raccoon that he had just shot on his bike, that was just as real.
That range of feelings poured into his work.

—HELEN FRANKENTHALER

The lower field in fall 1964 with Jo-Jo, the girls' oversized pony, and from left: *2 Circles 2 Crows*, 1963; *Cubi X*, 1963; and *Primo Piano I*, 1962. Photograph by David Smith.

The fields became more and more important, their design.
Often David would say, "Why don't you go out and photograph the fields?"
And he'd send me out.
The fields were his great vision,
truly long before anyone knew what he was up to.

— DAN BUDNIK

David Smith shows his nude paintings
in the new painting studio in May 1965.
Photograph by Alexander Liberman.

Untitled, 1963. Black egg ink on Japanese paper.
15½" x 20½" (39.4 x 52.1 cm).
The Collection of Candida and Rebecca Smith.

Working in the drawing studio in the house. Photograph by Dan Budnik.

He made his life around sculpture and I think he taught me that.
He said, "I pay a lot of money for paper—two dollars a sheet.
(This was a tremendous amount of money in those days. I was using lining paper to draw on.)
"I get the best paper to draw on. I don't care about creature comforts,
I care about sculpture having first claim on my money.
That's something you've got to sort of get right in your life."
That was good for me mentally; that's something we weren't used to in England. It was a lesson.

—ANTHONY CARO

Untitled, 1962. Ink and paint spray on paper,
11½" × 17½" (29.2 × 44.5 cm).
The Collection of Candida and Rebecca Smith.

From the Chelsea Series, 1960.
Black egg ink on paper, 26" × 40" (66 × 101.6 cm).
The Collection of Candida and Rebecca Smith.

Untitled, 1962. Black ink on paper,
19" × 24½" (48.3 × 62.2 cm).
The Collection of Candida and Rebecca Smith.

Untitled, 1963.
Spray enamel and white gouache on paper,
16¼" x 11½" (41.3 x 29.2 cm).
The Collection of Candida and Rebecca Smith.

Untitled, 1962.
Spray paint on paper,
13" x 19" (33 x 48.3 cm).
Private collection.

March 7, 1962, 1962.
Spray paint on paper, 18" x 22¾" (45.7 x 57.8 cm).
The Collection of Candida and Rebecca Smith.

The upper field during snowfall with groupings in rows of Voltri-Boltons, Voltons, and V.B.s, Cubis, and Circles, with the white-painted sculptures *Untitled* and *Circle and Box* in the foreground, both 1963. Photograph by Dan Budnik.

View of the 1997 exhibition with, from left to right: *Voltri-Bolton III*, 1962; *Lunar Arc*, 1961; *XI Books III Apples*, 1959; *The Sitting Printer*, 1954–55; and *Primo Piano III*, 1962. Photograph by Jerry L. Thompson.

The Fields at Storm King

The Fields at Storm King

CANDIDA N. SMITH

When Ralph Ogden visited Bolton Landing in 1966, he had a moment of epiphany that resulted in the world's quintessential sculpture park. Ogden negotiated the purchase for Storm King Art Center of the largest concentration of David Smith's sculptures in any museum collection, with representative works from many periods and series.

At Storm King Art Center we set out to create for the visitor a distinct and in-depth evocation of my father's sculpture fields—his vision, his environment. The fields of David Smith were a changing, growing process. In order to present this dynamic manifestation of his art, we decided to explore particular themes in layers over time. The themes were the circle, the figure in landscape, and the rich variations in surfaces in Smith's sculpture. Thus we decided on the unorthodox approach of a three-year, changing exhibition. Storm King's own extraordinary collection of David Smith's sculpture would be presented each year, and the themes in each sculpture would be explored by the addition of other works from museums, private collections, and the Collection of Candida and Rebecca Smith. I had once heard a dear friend of all of ours, Dick Bellamy, say of Storm King's collection of Smith's works, "It's a tough group, but I think I'm beginning to get it." Thus a goal was to make the context of each piece perfectly lucid to all viewers.

The three-year collaboration between Storm King Art Center and the family of David Smith in mounting "The Fields of David Smith" represents an extraordinary reach for the ineffable. For years we have asked ourselves: What were the fields? What did they mean? What did they mean to David Smith? How have they changed the encounter with sculpture?

In this exhibition we pursue these questions but offer no analytic solution. The drawings, paintings, and smaller-scale sculptures my father lived with inside his home and the large work set in the fields were a vital part of his creative process. Our intent is to give the viewer an opportunity to see his work as he saw it and to enter into his own process. The three-year period of the exhibition has allowed us to illustrate the changing nature of the original fields: the way certain sculptures changed position in the field, the way new work was added, and older work returned to lend special suggestiveness.

The selection and deployment of work follows historical placement as documented

1998 exhibition view with, from left: *The Woman Bandit*, 1956–58; *Sentinel V*, 1959; *Personage of May*, 1957; *Noland's Blues*, 1961; and *Three Ovals Soar*, 1960. Photograph by Jerry L. Thompson.

in photographs and an intuitive balancing of themes, surfaces, and tones, based on my own recollections.

Inside the museum building we placed smaller works near windows so they can be viewed in relation to the sculpture outdoors. The viewer can see that in Smith's oeuvre, monumentality is a characteristic completely independent of size. *Lonesome Man* (1957, in a photograph by David Smith, p. 126), *Royal Incubator* (1949, p. 70), and *Egg Temple* (1960, p. 95) were monumental works that David Smith photographed as such, despite their small scale. Drawings and paintings elucidate the artist's feelings about the form in landscape and, according to Smith's own metaphor, the artist in the world. In flat work he could also explore elements of mass, balance, and patterns of elusive form impossible to pursue in three dimensions. My father often painted his thoughts out.

Photographs interspersed throughout the exhibition bring us back again and again to the world as seen by David Smith: his work, his home, his fields. Some were taken by Smith himself, others by friends who were and are extremely gifted photographers: Dan Budnik, Alexander Liberman, and Harry Gitlin. Each photograph offers an entrance to the visitor. For the catalogue, Jerry L. Thompson photographed the works as shown at Storm King, in the many dramatically changing conditions of weather and light.

Storm King Art Center is the experiential sculpture museum. The visitor is freed from academic intermediaries to walk its five hundred acres and encounter sculpture one to one. In keeping with this spirit, we include personal reminiscences in this book, no dogma. As Irving Sandler reminds us, my father distrusted the wiles of words. That is how we present to you "The Fields of David Smith" at Storm King Art Center: no lines, no crowds, but all the time in the world to look, to reflect, and to find your own thoughts as you enter directly into my father's "work stream."

In each of the three years of the exhibition, the installations reflected groups of works that were in fact in the Bolton Landing fields. But we also chose a focus of emphasis for each particular year. In addition, we always included work relating to the themes of the other years. In this way, we hoped to build an overall image as the installations merged in memory, and to produce a faithful representation of David Smith's achievement.

The ample windows and glass doors of the museum building reminded me of those in the house at Bolton Landing in their effect of presenting the view outdoors and that within simultaneously. And so we paired works in the building with those in the landscape, just as my father had done with small works, drawings, and paintings,

XI Books III Apples, 1959. Stainless steel, 7'10" X 35" X 16¼" (2.39 x .89 x .41 m)
Storm King Art Center, Gift of the Ralph E. Ogden Foundation.
Photograph by Jerry L. Thompson.

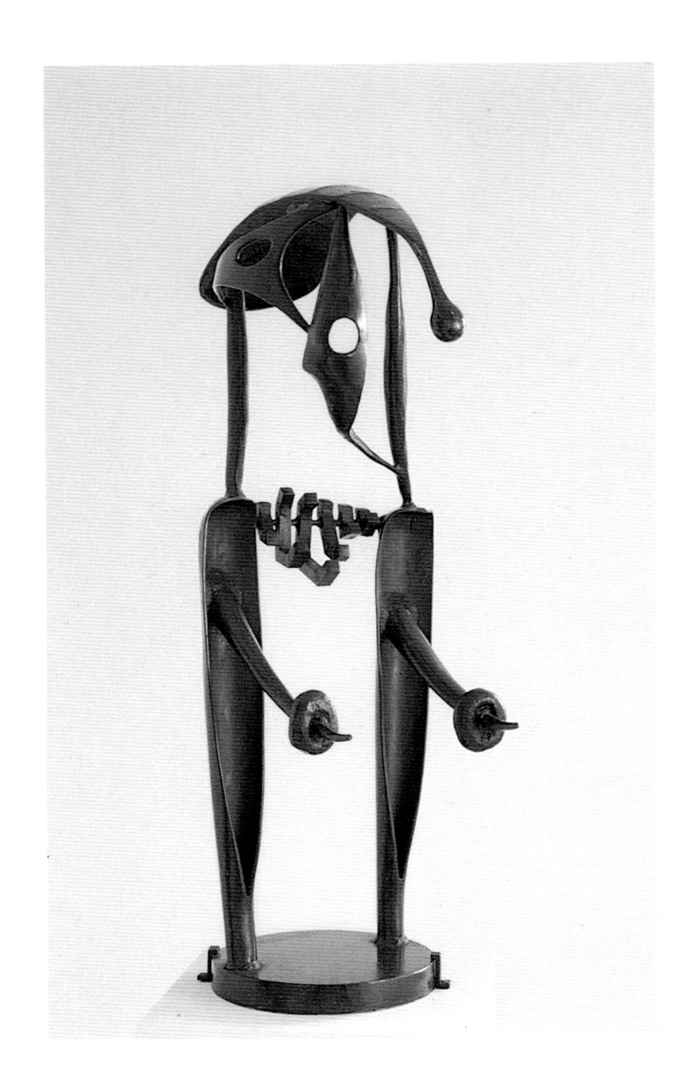

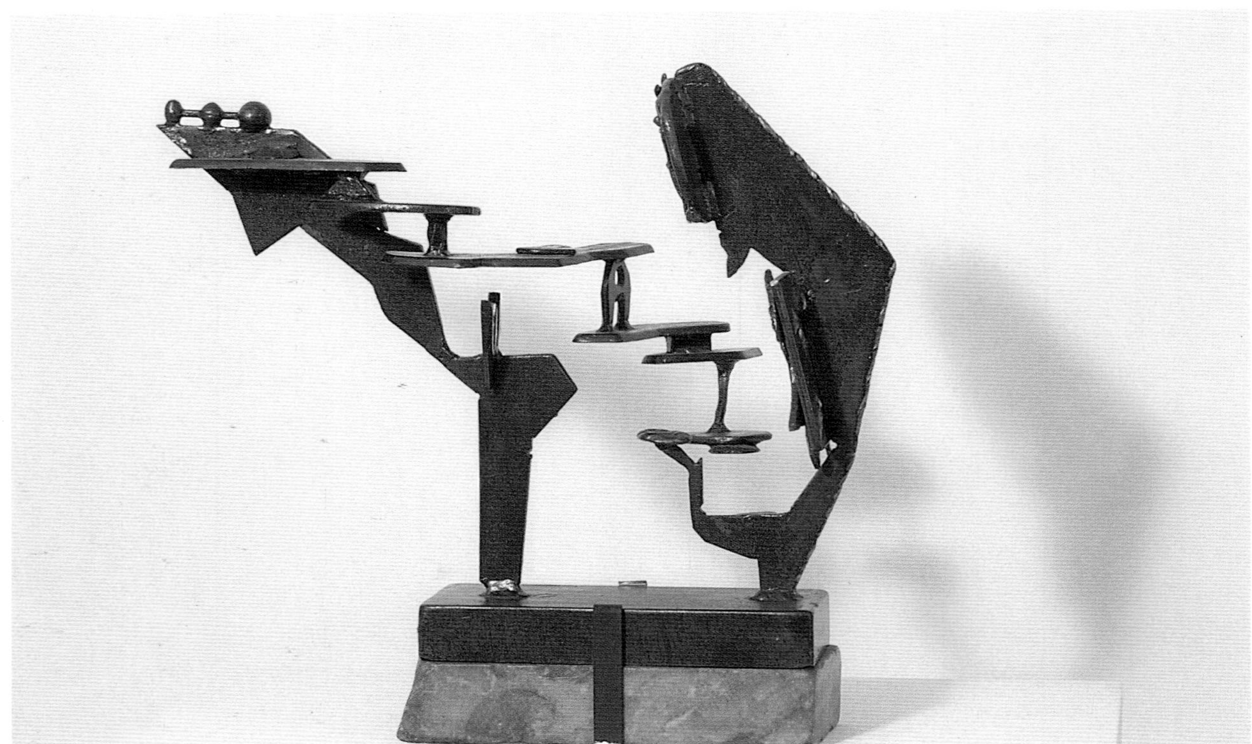

Works from the interior shows in 1997 and 1998.
Top, left: *Portrait of the Eagle's Keeper*, 1948–49. Steel and bronze, 39¼ × 12⅞ × 22" (99.70 × 37.70 × 55.88 cm). Collection of Helen Frankenthaler.
Right: *Royal Incubator*, 1949. Steel, bronze, and silver, 37⅛ × 39½ × 9⅞" Collection of Bagley and Virginia Wright.
Bottom: *Landscape with Strata*, 1946. Steel, bronze, and stainless steel on marble base, sculpture: 16½ × 19½ × 9¼" (41.91 × 49.53 × 23.50 cm), base: 2½ × 4⅛ × 10⅜" (6.35 × 10.44 × 26.35 cm). The Collection of Dr. and Mrs. Arthur E. Kahn.

Installation view of the 1998 exhibition with, outdoors at left: *Personage of May*, 1957. Bronze, 71⅝ × 31½ × 18½" (181.93 × 80.01 × 46.99 cm). Storm King Art Center, Gift of the Ralph E. Ogden Foundation.
At right: *Detroit Queen*, 1957. Bronze, 71¾ × 22¼ × 24⅜" (182.25 × 56.52 × 61.91 cm). Fogg Art Museum, Harvard University Art Museums, Gift of Lois Orswell. Photographs by Jerry L. Thompson.

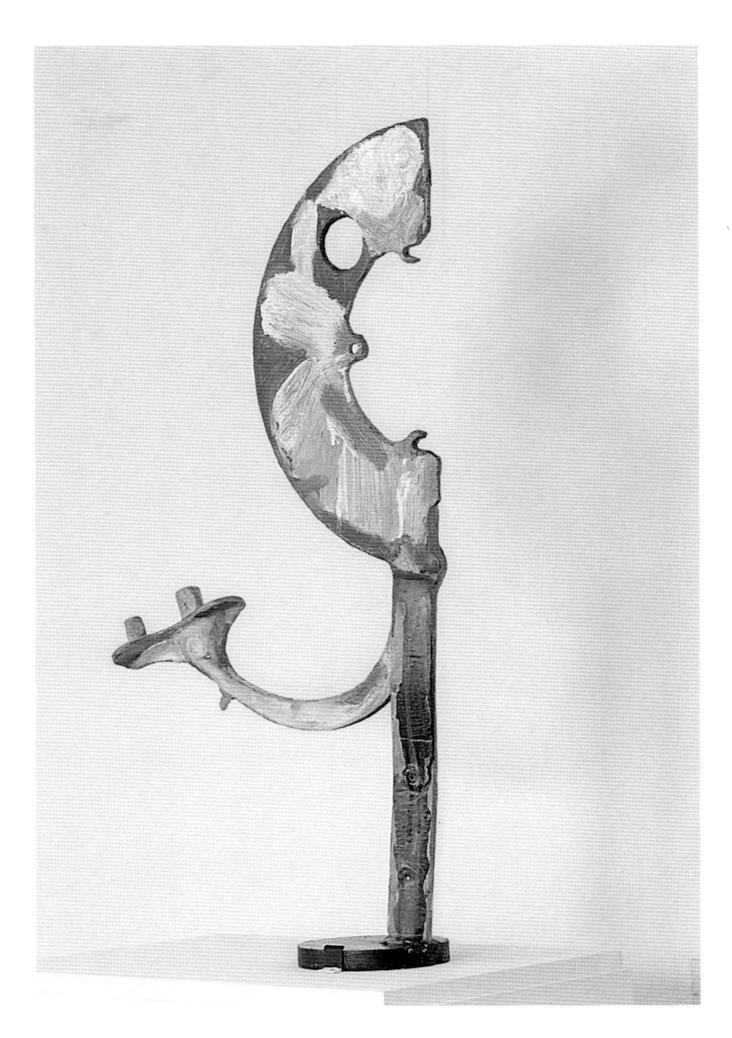

Untitled, 1958–59.
Steel and cast iron painted various colors,
30¾ × 20 × 5½" (78.11 × 50.80 × 13.97 cm).

Menand VII, 1963.
Steel painted green, 22¾ × 16⅛ × 12" (57.79 × 40.92 × 30.48 cm).
Both smaller works the Collection of Candida
and Rebecca Smith. Photographs by Jerry L. Thompson.

Lunar Arc, 1961. Steel painted white, 11'2" × 48" × 18" (3.40 × 1.22 × .46 cm).
Donald L. Bryant, Jr. Family Trust. Photograph by Jerry L. Thompson.

Crew installing *Volton XVIII*, 1963, for the 1997 Storm King show. Photograph by Jerry L. Thompson.

which he kept around and available to his eye. At times we used the exact works that had been in the house; at others we used works to reinforce and explicate outdoor themes. We also interspersed historical photographs of the fields with Smith's art-work to remind the viewer again and again of the original context. In some instances considerations of conservation led us to place works in the galleries; many years after their creation, some sculptures can no longer be safely exposed to the elements.

1997

Long before any sculptures arrived at Storm King, preparations began. Outdoor bases were fabricated by the same method David Smith used. Peter Stevens, my

Smith positioning the piece
in the lower field at Bolton Landing
in October or November 1963.
Photograph by Dan Budnik.

brother-in-law and administrator of the Collection of Candida and Rebecca Smith, had done the research into and analysis of this technique. David Collens, Director of Storm King, had pored over historical photographs with a magnifying glass, analyzing Smith's technique and planning how best to adapt it for our installation. With Peter Stevens's help, Collens devised a plan. During the winter neither we nor my father could have sunk a base into frozen ground. So, during the early spring, rough wooden molds were constructed and filled with cement, gravel, and rocks in specific proportions. The resulting surface is crude yet natural.

David Collens designed pedestals that were sunk much more deeply into the earth than Smith's had been, for added stability. I was deeply grateful for this precaution when fourteen straight days of rain came just before the 1998 opening. Our precious

Detail of *Volton XX*, 1963, in the 1997 show. Steel, 62½ x 34 x 29" (158.75 x 86.36 x 73.66 cm).
Storm King Art Center, Gift of the Ralph E. Ogden Foundation.
Photograph by Jerry L. Thompson.

tonnage of cement and sculpture held secure. Collens also added a useful refinement, handles placed just below ground level so that Storm King's big machinery could pluck eight-hundred-pound blocks out of their beds effortlessly.

These bases required weeks of preparation and drying before they could be planted, but fewer than in my father's time. (Smith had built the molds directly in the ground, while at Storm King the molds were built and the bases cast in the workshop.) Independent construction of the bases and a large and skilled work crew made the difference. My father had usually worked with a few men from the local road crew or with farmers returning favors. We, on the other hand, had trained art movers, special equipment, and conservators on call. Still, it requires experience and intuition to understand the weight spread and key points on a sculpture to move it safely. It is a tricky business. Once sculptures were rooted safely in place, the grounds crew rolled sod seamlessly, camouflaging the disturbed ground.

We sited the outdoor work in a way that departed from traditional museum installation. We began with photographed images of the sculptures mounted on stick bases, which we set up on tables outside. We needed to consider trees, vistas, and the fall of the land. David Collens's passion for Storm King is such that, to him, the landscape is a living, growing being. He knows intimately the paths of light as they occur during the day and the seasonal journeys of those paths. He knows the changes of verdure as the summer comes and which branches must come down in order to maintain views. Collens possesses a strong and specific feeling about each spot and vista at Storm King. His knowledge was vital to the installation, as was that of William Rutherford, Storm King's landscape designer. From Peter Stern, Chairman and President of the Art Center, we received unstinting support and encouragement. The Smith family and the Storm King team worked as one with the single goal of the cultivation of "The Fields of David Smith."

As work arrived it was uncrated and, when necessary, treated with a gentle protective coating. Condition was always checked by conservators. We used flagged markers to begin to place the work in space. We considered the historical relationships of certain sculptures, and placed those close to each other. Sculptures that had stood near the pond at Bolton Landing we sited in areas of dappled light, attempting as much as possible to achieve an evocation of their original placement. Once we proposed a spot for a work, I would stand in that spot, sensing its spatial requirements and the effect upon it of other sculptures. My relationships with my father's sculptures are almost those of a sibling. I feel, for example, one's bravery, another's poignancy. This intimate connection helped me immensely in making decisions about the deployment of the entire group.

Smith and his assistant, Leon Pratt, and crew installing *Primo Piano III*, 1962, in the upper field at Bolton Landing in October or November of 1963 (with *Circle II*, 1962, at rear).

Smith checking the level on *Primo Piano III* after installation, with *Primo Piano II*, 1962, at left, and *Circle I*, 1962, at rear. Photographs by Dan Budnik.

Once the outdoor "mapping" of the exhibition was complete, we moved indoors, where we arranged works to interact with the window views that accompanied them.

Each of the exhibition's three years reflected a different emphasis in viewing David Smith's sculptures. In the opening year, 1997, we explored the proud, audacious diversity of surface and theme that my father had always in mind as he worked on many pieces at the same time.

Each year the exhibition began with the small center gallery, where we installed an early, seminal work—an underpinning image. Smith once wrote that he had time only to explore ideas he had had up through the 1920s and 1930s. *Landscape with Strata* (1946, p. 70) shows a multilayered land peopled with sculpture. *Royal Incubator* (1949, p. 70) expresses a grandeur of vision in which sculptural forms define a world. These pieces, then, define in small form the vision behind the outdoor monumental sculptures and their effect on us and the landscape they inhabit.

Close to each other and close to the house stood *Circle and Box* and its *Untitled* companion, both 1963 (pp. 86–87, 89), just as they stood at Bolton Landing (p. 63). The fiercely figural group of Voltons (1963) and Voltri-Boltons (1962–63), which patrolled the far periphery of the upper field in Bolton Landing (pp. 42, 62–63), were brought closer in and integrated with more planar, abstract pieces like *Primo Piano III* of 1962 (p. 83). We needed to telescope the space while maintaining the original dynamic balance of the aspects of the artist's identity. Thus, *Primo Piano III* and *Lunar Arc* (1961, pp. 64–65) again stood against a distant mountain view, punching out a still, white shape against the natural action of the landscape. The lyrical lift of *Study in Arcs* (1957, p. 97) hovered against trees and sky. *Three Ovals Soar* (1960, p. 108) brought the play of light onto stainless steel into its rising dance. In contrast, the bright flat-painted *2 Circle IV* (1962, p. 88) stood upright, its stacked blue and yellow circles revealing far distances in its cutout openings. Its spatial reverse, *2 Circles 2 Crows* (1963, p. 86), made of the cutout shapes employed horizontally with a painted white circle around each, was sited nearby at Storm King. At Bolton Landing, they occupied different fields (pp. 42 and 51, 57), but we took this liberty to clarify their relationship for the viewer and to make the difference in their action more dramatic. *Rebecca Circle* (1961, p. 119) stood out against the land like a wildflower. Its vibrant colors and their painterly application are an abstraction from nature. *Lunar Arc* (p. 72) could be seen from indoors through the windows of a room dedicated to it, with related sculptures, spray paintings, and photographs.

The indoor silver *Books and Apple* (1957, p. 133) was related to the abstract still life *XI Books III Apples* (1959, p. 68), which was shown outdoors. Along with the stainless steel circle *Untitled* (1964, p. 134), they looked forward to the third and final year's emphasis on stainless steel.

Thus we included surfaces of rusted metal, flat painted color, flat white, bronze, and stainless steel. The theme of circles reflects Smith's unending interest in that form.

1998

In 1998, the second year of the exhibition, we continued to consider the surfaces of David Smith's sculpture, but with an emphasis on bronze. We explored the artist's profound interest in the figure by gathering a formidable group of his "portraits." We began with the *Portrait of the Eagle's Keeper* (1948–49), with its stern and regal tone, and *Royal Incubator* (1949, both p. 70), which describes the turbulence of a powerfully infused space, and proceeded from there with a series sometimes graphic and frightening—*Portrait of a Lady Painter* (1954; 1956–57, pp. 98–99)—sometimes witty—*The Woman Bandit* (1956–58, p. 100)—or delicately poignant—*Portrait of a Young Girl* (1954, not reproduced)—surrealistically grand and classical—*Auburn Queen* (1959, p. 121) and *Detroit Queen* (1957, pp. 71, 120)—or starkly personal—*Pilgrim* (1957, not reproduced) and *Portrait of a Painter* (1954, p. 101). The great adventure lay in seeing this group together, so many of them walking forward, extending a foot in midstride.

Smith often used found objects not made of metal, which he covered with plaster and then cast in bronze (thus softening the lines and tailoring the object precisely to his intention). This technique appears in many of these bronze works, and especially clearly in *The Sitting Printer* (1954–55, detail p. 94).

Photographs taken in the spring of 1965, shortly before my father's death, show *Personage of May* (1957) front and center in the lower field (p. 120). We placed it so at Storm King; a brave, bronze-cloaked scarecrow. Set against the most distant vista were the *Untitled* (*Candida*) of 1965 (p. 135), its stainless steel panels reflecting the sun's changing light and referring to the emphasis of the exhibition of the year to come, and *2 Circle IV* (1962, p. 88), a reminder of the installation of the previous year. *Voltri-Bolton X* (1962, pp. 104, 105) relates to another of our themes in that it forms a circle of found steel shards surmounted by rays of tongs. *Sentinel V* (1959, pp. 108–109) is a figure in landscape and also an abstract and heroic portrait of the artist's stance in the world.

On Storm King's east lawn we brought together three closely related works: *Hi Candida* (1965) and *Becca* and *Construction December II,* both 1964 (pp. 102–103). They are abstract, rusted-steel, improvisational compositions that look like piles of steel tossed into the air, weightless and frozen in time. In fact, they are brilliantly crafted constructions. Even the rusting process, which in Smith's work appears casual, was carefully controlled with protective treatments. Sometimes, when the rust failed to add the desired color, Smith subtly in-painted reds, browns, and oranges.

The three sculptures were installed with other resolutely abstract works (pp. 4–5; 112–113): *Primo Piano II* (1962), *Oval Node* and *Untitled* (both 1963), *Voltri VIII* and *Voltri XVI* (both 1962), and *Primo Piano III* (1962). (We felt it was important for visitors to see Voltris outdoors with other work, as Smith had never had the opportunity to do.) *Primo Piano II* draws together several themes; the architectonic horizontality of the Primo Pianos, the use of the circle, and the surfaces of stainless steel, bronze, and steel painted flat white. *Rebecca Circle* and *Dida's Circle on a Fungus* (both 1961) were re-united and placed in their old relation to each other and in their original Bolton Landing position on the far edge of the field (pp. 116–119).

In Storm King's only gallery that does not look out onto our exhibition area, we showed a special group of pieces made of five equally sized stacked objects: *Five Units Equal* (1956), *V.B. XXII* (1963), and *Egg Temple* (1960, p. 95). The formal similarity, rich surfaces, and evocative variety of this group speak of the utter mastery of the sculptor. Using the abstract idea of five shapes stacked, he managed to evoke dramatically different effects.

The long upstairs gallery, which I had come to think of as the "atelier," held *Personage from Stove City* (1946, not reproduced), a work that spent years on our Bolton Landing terrace, and other small works that we kept in the house during the great years of the sculpture fields. Here we showed what I call the "small-scale monumentals" through which Smith proved that monumentality need have no relation to size.

We also showed *Three Planes* (1960–61, not reproduced), constructed of one black painted vertical element with a red plane and a white plane on diagonals. It was always a favorite of mine, although I had not seen it since one late summer day in 1963. My father asked my sister and me what were our favorite sculptures, and did we want to take anything back to our mother's house with us. I said, "That one," and pointed to *Three Planes*, which stood just away from the terrace garden. It was much too large for our small home so he made a miniature and sent it to me very soon thereafter. I was very happy but wondered why he had changed the red element to orange. I still do.

Primo Piano III, 1962, as sited in the 1997 Storm King show.
Steel painted white, 10'5" x 12'1" x 18" (31.8 x 3.68 x .46 cm).
The Collection of Candida and Rebecca Smith. Photograph by Jerry L. Thompson.

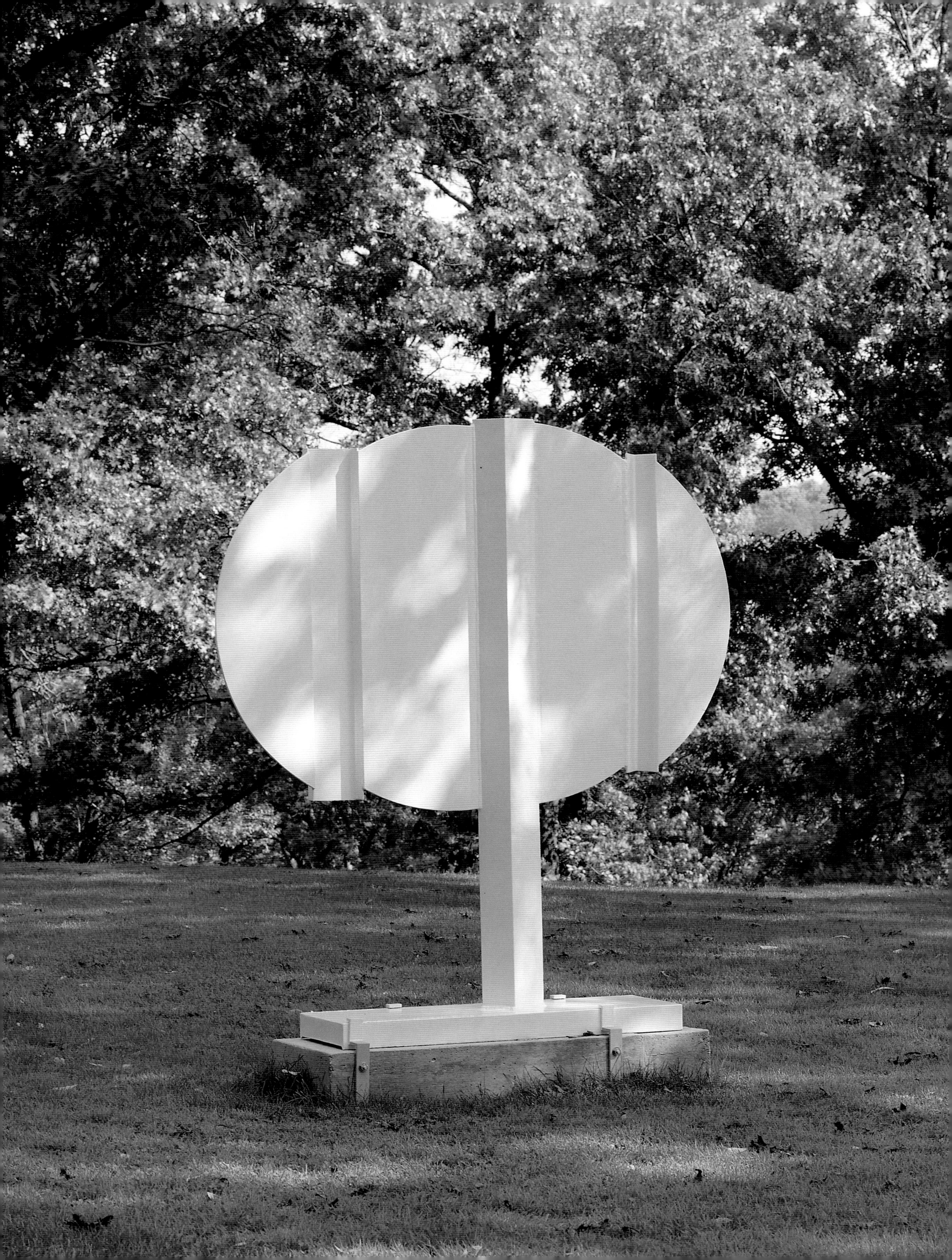

Oval Node, 1963.
Steel painted white, 8' x 7'1" x 18" (2.44 x 2.16 x .46 cm).
The Collection of Candida and Rebecca Smith.

Primo Piano II, 1962.
Steel painted white, stainless steel, and bronze,
7'5⅝" x 13'4¾" x 32⅞" (2.28 x 4.08 x .84 cm).
The Collection of Candida and Rebecca Smith,
on loan to the French Nation,
installation de sculptures du XXième siècle
dans le jardin des Tuileries à Paris.
Photographs by Jerry L. Thompson.

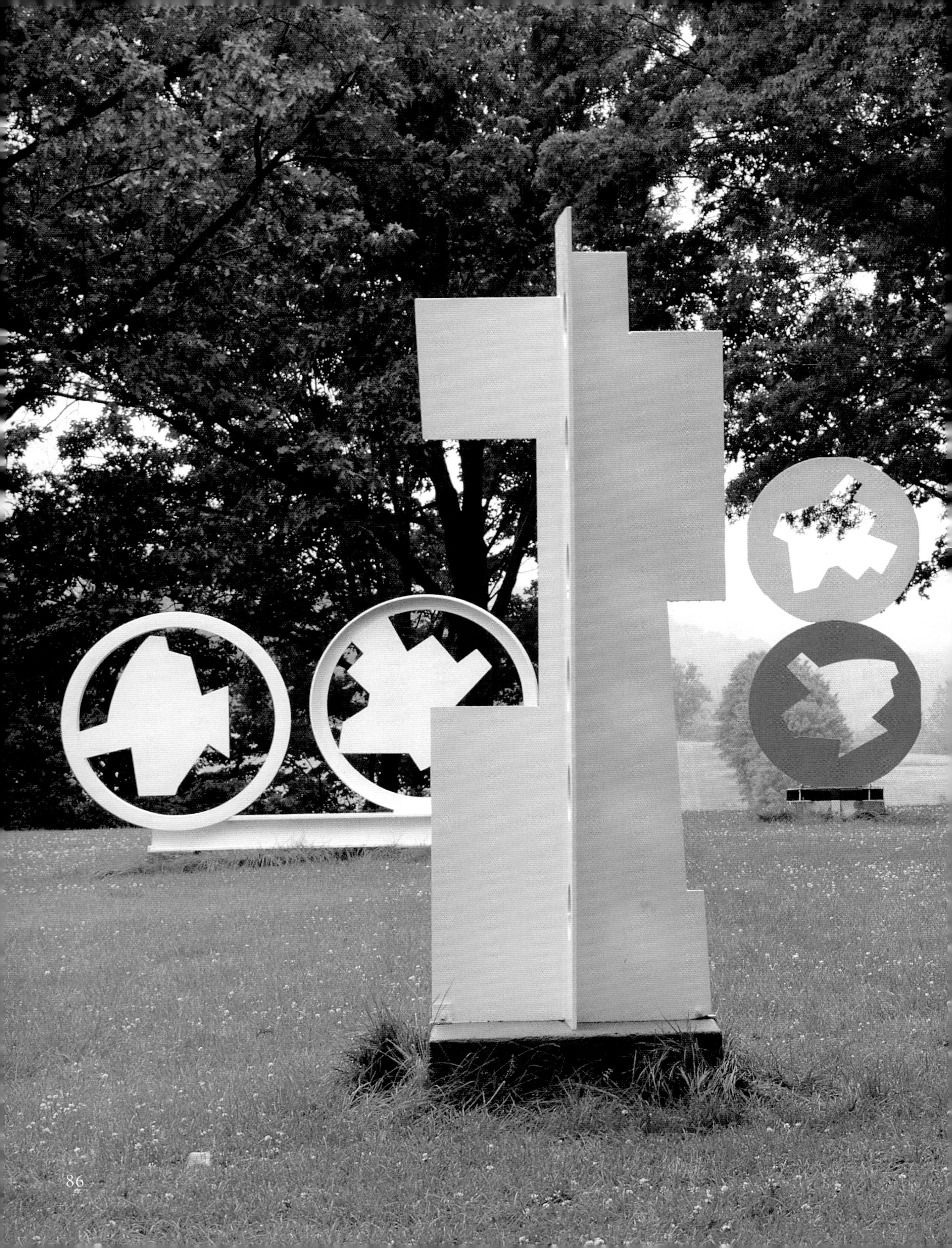

View of the 1997 exhibition with, from left, foreground: *Untitled* and *Circle and Box*, both 1963, and in background: *2 Circles 2 Crows*, 1963, and *2 Circle IV*, 1962. Photograph by Jerry L. Thompson.

2 Circle IV, 1962, as sited in the 1997 exhibition. Steel painted yellow and blue, 9'11⅞" x 65¼" x 28¼" (3.04 x 1.66 x .72 m). The Collection of Mr. and Mrs. David N. Pincus. Photograph by Jerry L. Thompson.

At left: *Untitled*, 1963.
Steel painted white,
7'4" x 33" x 26" (2.24 x .84 x .66 m).
The Collection of Candida
and Rebecca Smith.
Right: *Circle and Box*, 1963.
Steel painted white,
9'11½" x 29¼" x 22½" (3.04 x .74 x .57 m).
The Collection of Irma
and Norman Braman.
Photograph by Jerry L. Thompson.

Details of *Voltri-Bolton III*, 1962,
and *Volton XX*, 1963.
Photographs by Jerry L. Thompson.

The Sitting Printer, 1954–55, as photographed by David Smith against Lake George and as sited at Storm King and photographed by Jerry L. Thompson. Bronze, 7'3" x 15¾" x 17" (2.21 x .40 x .43 m). Storm King Art Center, Gift of the Ralph E. Ogden Foundation.

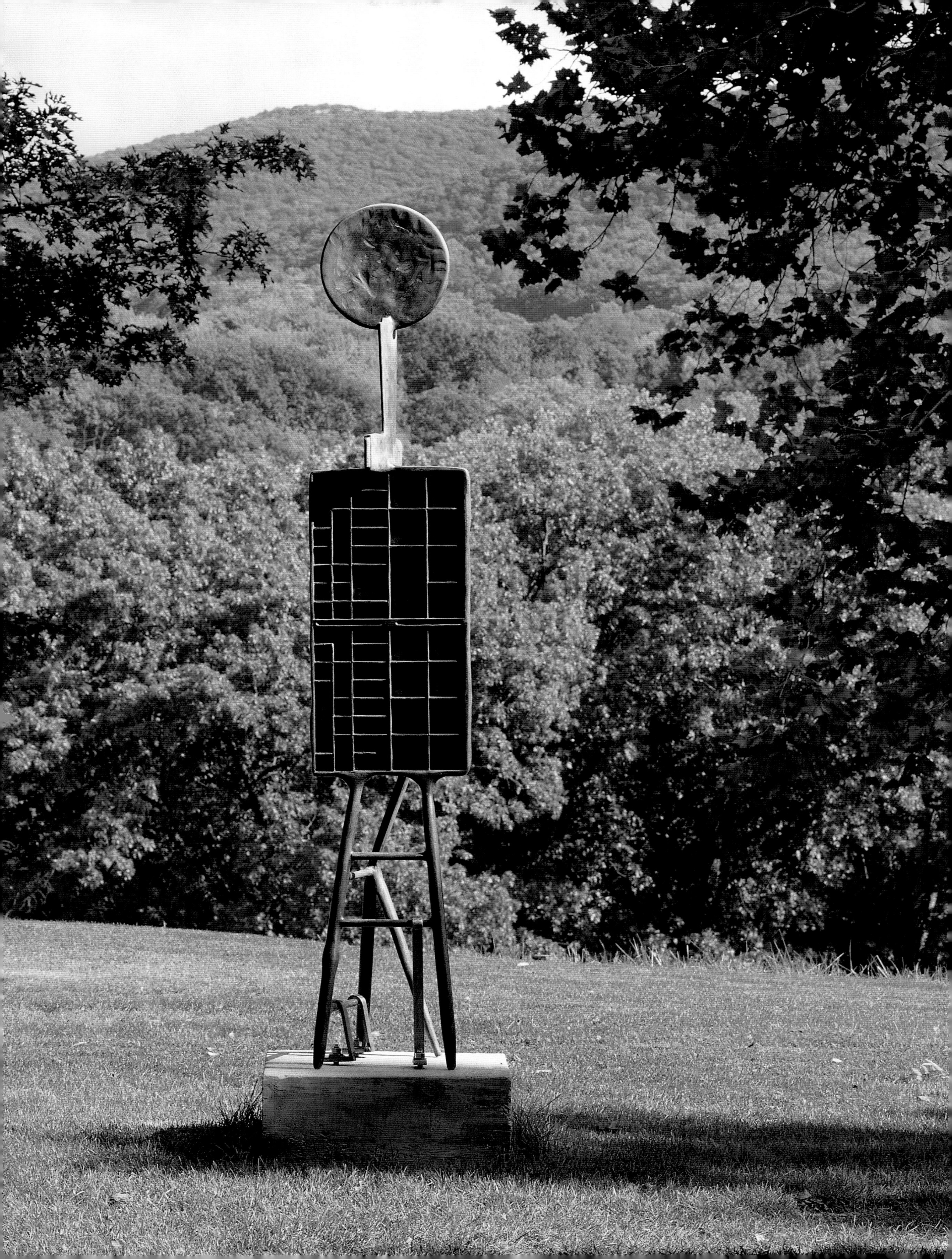

Three of the smaller-scale works shown indoors. From left to right: *V.B. XXII*, 1963. Steel, 8'3⅝" x 14¼" x 13" (2.53 x .36 x .33 m). Courtesy of the Museum of American Art of the Pennsylvania Academy of the Fine Arts, Gift of Mr. and Mrs. David N. Pincus.
Center: *Egg Temple*, 1960. Bronze, 20½ x 8¾ x 6¾" (52.07 x 22.23 x 17.15 cm). Collection of Leonard and Adele Blumberg.
Right: *Five Units Equal*, 1956. Steel painted light green, 6'1¼" x 16" x 14" (1.86 x .41 x .36 m).
Storm King Art Center, Gift of the Ralph E. Ogden Foundation.

Opposite: detail of *The Sitting Printer*, 1954–55. Photographs by Jerry L. Thompson.

View of the 1998 exhibition with, from left: *Study in Arcs*, 1957; *XI Books III Apples*, 1959;
The Woman Bandit, 1956–58; *Personage of May*, 1957;
Sentinel V, 1959;
Three Ovals Soar, 1960; and *Noland's Blues*, 1961.
At right: *Study in Arcs*, 1957.
Steel painted pink, 11' x 9'6½" x 3'½" (3.35 x 2.91 x .93 m).
Storm King Art Center, Gift of the Ralph E. Ogden Foundation.
Photographs by Jerry L. Thompson.

Portrait of a Lady Painter, 1954; 1956–57,
detail and full view. Bronze, 64 × 59¾ × 12½" (162.56 × 151.77 × 31.75 cm).
Storm King Art Center, Gift of the Ralph E. Ogden Foundation.
Photographs by Jerry L. Thompson.

Above: *The Woman Bandit*, 1956–58. Cast iron, bronze, and steel, 68¼ x 12⅛ x 11½" (173.36 x 30.76 x 29.21 cm).
Right: *Portrait of a Painter*, 1954.
Bronze, 8'½" x 24¾" x 12" (2.45 x .63 x .30 m).
Both sculptures The Collection of Candida and Rebecca Smith. Photographs by Jerry L. Thompson.

View of the 1998 exhibition with, from left: *Hi Candida*, 1965.
Steel, 6'6½" x 7'10½" x 22½" (1.99 x 2.40 x .57 m).
Collection of Irma and Norman Braman.
Center: *Becca*, 1964. Steel, 6'6" x 47½" x 23½" (1.98 x 1.21 x .60 m).
Storm King Art Center, Gift of the Ralph E. Ogden Foundation.
Right: *Construction December II*, 1964.
Steel, 6'10¾" x 67½" x 30½" (2.10 x 1.71 x .77 m).
The Collection of Candida and Rebecca Smith.
Below: *Raven IV*, 1957. Steel, 27⅛ x 32⅛ x 13¼" (68.89 x 81.60 x 33.65 cm).
Hirshhorn Museum and Sculpture Garden, Smithsonian Institution.
Gift of Joseph H. Hirshhorn, 1966. Photographs by Jerry L. Thompson.

Voltri-Bolton X, 1962
Steel, 6'9" x 41" x 15" (1.80 x 1.04 x .38 cm).
Collection of Jerome and Ellen Stern.
Photographs by Jerry L. Thompson.

Voltri-Bolton III, 1962. Steel, 8' × 36⅞" × 13⅜" (2.44 × .94 × .33 m).
Right: *Volton XIII*, 1963. Steel, 7'1" × 25¾" × 18⅞" (2.16 × .65 × .50 m).
Both works The State of New York, Governor Nelson A. Rockefeller,
Empire State Plaza State Art Collection, Albany, New York. Photographs by Jerry L. Thompson.

Above: *Three Ovals Soar* and *Sentinel V*, as installed in the 1998 exhibition.
Three Ovals Soar, 1960. Stainless steel, 11'3½" x 31" x 23" (3.44 x .79 x .58 m).
Right: *Sentinel V*, 1959. Stainless steel, 12'2" x 47½" x 21" (3.71 x 1.21 x .53 m).
The Collection of Candida and Rebecca Smith,
courtesy National Gallery of Art, Washington, D. C.
Photographs by Jerry L. Thompson.

Left: *Hi Candida*, 1965. Steel, 6'6½" x 7'10½" x 22½" (1.99 x 2.40 x .57 m).
Collection of Irma and Norman Braman.
Above: *Voltri XVI*, 1962. Steel, 44 x 51½ x 34¾" (111.76 x 130.81 x 88.27 cm).
The Collection of Candida and Rebecca Smith. Photographs by Jerry L. Thompson.

The 1998 exhibition with, at left: *Untitled*, 1963. Steel painted white, 7'4" x 33" x 26" (2.24 x .84 x .66 m). The Collection of Candida and Rebecca Smith. *Voltri VIII*, 1962. Steel, 6'7⅛" x 41" x 33¾" (2.01 x 1.04 x .86 m). Collection of Mr. and Mrs. Harold P. Starr.
Above: *Voltri VIII; Hi Candida*, 1965; and *Construction December II*, 1964. Photographs by Jerry L. Thompson.

He spent a great deal of time in museums looking at the ancients.
And looking at the mistakes of others. He said, "You know, this is not all success.
I've learned a lot from the mistakes of others, and from my own mistakes too."
That's what it's all about: not success, success, but pushing into places we haven't seen before.
That's his gift to us; he's taken us to places we haven't seen before.

—DAN BUDNIK

View of the 1998 exhibition. Photograph by Jerry L. Thompson.

Two views of *Dida's Circle on a Fungus*, 1961, in the 1998 exhibition. Steel painted various colors, 8'4" x 47" x 24" (2.54 x 1.19 x .61 m). The Collection of Candida and Rebecca Smith. Above, with *Construction December II*, and *Becca*, both 1964, and *Voltri VIII*, 1962. Photographs by Jerry L. Thompson.

David seemed concerned with altering space,
rather than adapting to it.

— GEORGE RICKEY

Primo Piano II, 1962; *Dida's Circle on a Fungus*, 1961; and *Rebecca Circle*, 1961.
Steel painted various colors, 6'7" x 53" x 24" (2.01 x 1.35 x .61 m).
All works The Collection of Candida and Rebecca Smith.
As sited in the1998 exhibition. Photograph by Jerry L. Thompson.

Left: *V.B. XXII*, 1963, with *Untitled*, 1961.
Right: *Personage of May* and *Detroit Queen*, both 1957,
as photographed by David Smith at Bolton Landing in1957.
Facing page: *Auburn Queen*, 1959. Bronze, 7'2⅜" x 36" x 21⅝" (2.19 x .91 x .55 m).
Hirshhorn Museum and Sculpture Garden, Smithsonian Institution.
Gift of Joseph H. Hirshhorn, 1966.
V.B.XXII, Personage of May, Detroit Queen, and *Auburn Queen* were brought together again in the 1998 exhibition.
All photographs by David Smith.

Because of his ability to be the essential student, he goes back in circles in time,
in symbolism that we can all relate to in our conscious
and subconscious minds. It's in the bedrock. It doesn't age; it stays fresh.

— DAN BUDNIK

1999

At this writing, the 1998 exhibition still stands, splendidly backlit by the flaming colors of autumnal light and foliage. The final show, for 1999, remains a vision. Our emphasis will be on works in stainless steel and silver. David Smith created a technique, often copied, of burnishing stainless surfaces with paintbrush-like grinder marks, rendering them both durable and reflective, able to hold ambient colors of sky, grass, and the changing light of the sun. It is a way of "painting" with nature's colors. We will faithfully represent groups that stood primarily in the lower field during my father's last years, while at the same time demonstrating the dramatically different expressions of stainless steel. And we will visually delineate, for the first time in an exhibition, the relationship between the silver and the stainless steel sculptures.

In 1954 David Smith began to work extensively with silver, using materials supplied by a commission from Towle Silversmiths. We include *Egyptian Barnyard* (1954, not reproduced) along with the earlier steel *Stainless Window* (1951, p. 55), both landscape "drawings in space." Later, in 1957, after Smith had been extending his use of stainless steel, he became challenged by the difficulties of cutting and welding this material with the technology available at the time. Smith reverted to silver for an exquisite series of small monumental sculptures all made in 1957. While these are neither studies nor maquettes for the large stainless sculptures, they relate immediately to them. Smith was thinking about the big works. He did his best thinking while at work.

Continuing to pair indoor and outdoor pieces, we will see the silver *Tower Eight* (1957, p. 128) with the stainless steel *Tower I* (1963, p. 129). While both are figural and soaring, the sinuousness of *Tower I* is achieved without a single curve. The silver *Books and Apple* (1957) will be seen with *XI Books III Apples* (1959, p. 68) and *Cubi V* (1963, p. 133), reflecting a tension between still life and the figure that brings an immediacy and sense of motion to the composition of geometric forms. The exquisite silver self-portrait *Lonesome Man* (1957, p. 126) stands in a poetic relation to *Sentinel V* (1959, p. 109) and *Superstructure on 4* (1960, p. 127). *Horse* (1961, p. 136) is a made-to-scale silver copy of a paper assemblage made by my sister, Rebecca. It surely was the impetus for the large, flat *Becca* (1964) and *Untitled (Candida)* of 1965, both constructions of flat planar elements (pp. 137; 135). We will also exhibit many examples from Smith's greatly admired Cubi series together with early works that foreshadow these stainless steel sculptures built primarily of volumetric Cubist elements. For example, the stainless steel and wrought iron *Aggressive Character* (1947, p. 131) will be shown with a small painting from the 1930s that my sister Rebecca and Peter Stevens have nicknamed "Cubi on My Mind." It shows a head in profile with cubic constructions inside the brain cavity.

As photographed by David Smith in Spoleto, Italy, shortly after completion:
Voltri V, 1962. Steel, 7'2⅝" x 39½" x 21¾" (2.20 x 1.00 x .54 m).
Hirshhorn Museum and Sculpture Garden, Smithsonian Institution.
Gift of Joseph H. Hirshhorn, 1966.

View of the 1998 exhibition with *Oval Node*, 1963,
and *Primo Piano II*, 1962.
Photograph by Jerry L. Thompson.

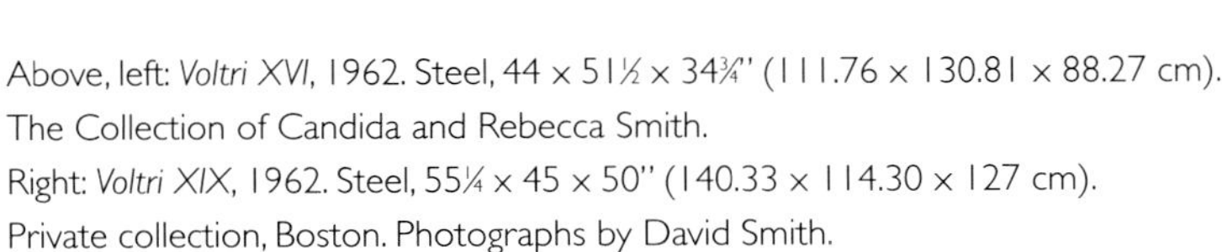

Above, left: *Voltri XVI*, 1962. Steel, 44 x 51½ x 34¾" (111.76 x 130.81 x 88.27 cm). The Collection of Candida and Rebecca Smith.
Right: *Voltri XIX*, 1962. Steel, 55¼ x 45 x 50" (140.33 x 114.30 x 127 cm). Private collection, Boston. Photographs by David Smith.

Smith's painted Circle series is well known from the permanent installation at the National Gallery of Art, Washington, D.C. We will show less familiar stainless circles in their original role as lenses. At Storm King these elegant, spare works will target nature and parts of their fellow sculptures, just as they did at Bolton Landing. We will explore Smith's interest in arcs, which he thought of as slices of circles and disks. *Lunar Arc* (1961) is a piece of the rim of a circle. The arcs in *Three Ovals Soar* (1960), *Study in Arcs* (1957), and *Lunar Arcs on Leg* (1956–60) are slices of the inside of a cresent—the arc we see on the inner edge of a new moon. Our examination of the Voltri series continues with *Voltri V, Voltri XVI,* and the triumphant *Voltri XIX,* all 1962. Because Smith's work is so often associated with the figure, I like to balance this view with sculptures that are about dwelling places, such as Voltris XVI and XIX (1962, p. 125), in which workbenches describe the place where a sculptor truly lives, and the Primo Pianos of 1962, which refer to the main floor of a dwelling.

My father felt a ferocious pride in his work. With "belligerent affection," he wrestled his materials from a parsimonious world; he fashioned the work with extreme physical labor; he defended it from onslaughts by critics, collectors, museums, prize panels, and art dealers. The ensuing conflicts were baffling to many but sprung simply from his own respect for his art and the expectation of a similar respect from others. Seen together as a great current of my father's work stream, these structures from our fields resume their flow uninterrupted in the fields of Storm King. I can feel his vitality and conviction, not only as memory, but here as a fresh experience.

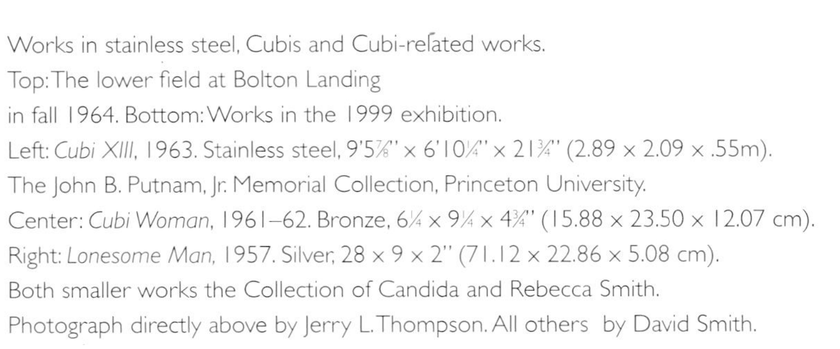

Works in stainless steel, Cubis and Cubi-related works.
Top: The lower field at Bolton Landing
in fall 1964. Bottom: Works in the 1999 exhibition.
Left: *Cubi XIII*, 1963. Stainless steel, 9'5⅞" × 6'10¼" × 21¾" (2.89 × 2.09 × .55m).
The John B. Putnam, Jr. Memorial Collection, Princeton University.
Center: *Cubi Woman*, 1961–62. Bronze, 6¼ × 9¼ × 4¾" (15.88 × 23.50 × 12.07 cm).
Right: *Lonesome Man*, 1957. Silver, 28 × 9 × 2" (71.12 × 22.86 × 5.08 cm).
Both smaller works the Collection of Candida and Rebecca Smith.
Photograph directly above by Jerry L. Thompson. All others by David Smith.

Left: *Superstructure on 4*, 1960. Stainless steel, 11' 7¾" x 6' 7¾" x 22" (3.55 x 2.03 x .56 m).
University of Nebraska, Lincoln. Bequests of Frances Sheldon and Adams Bromley Sheldon, 1969. Photograph by David Smith.
Right: *Cubi III*, 1961. Stainless steel, 7' 11¾" x 33" x 19" (2.43 x .83 x .48 m). Museum of Contemporary Art, Los Angeles.
Partial gift of Beatrice and Philip Gersh. Photograph by Peter Stevens.
Superstructure on 4 exhibited in the 1999 exhibition.

Any great sculpture has a certain poise; it's lifted up and out, and balanced, part of the ground but also part of heaven. His best sculptures have this. Part of his gesture was a kind of magnificent clumsiness, which I honor in all art, whether it's in Courbet or Rodin or anybody. We feel that this is so off, in a way, and so inventive, and so great.

—HELEN FRANKENTHALER

Tower Eight, 1957. Silver, 46½ x 13 x 10" (118.11 x 33.02 x 25.40 cm). The Patsy R. and Raymond D. Nasher Collection, Dallas, Texas.

Tower I, 1963. Stainless steel, 23'6" x 34" x 36" (7.16 x .86 x .91 m).
The Collection of Candida and Rebecca Smith.
Both works exhibited in the 1999 exhibition.
Photographs by David Smith.

Cubis in the 1999 exhibition, from left to right: *Cubi I,* 1963.
Stainless steel, 10'4" x 34½" x 33½". The Detroit Institute of Arts,
Founders Society Purchase, Special Purchase Fund.
Cubi XXIV, 1964. Stainless steel, 9'6½" x 7'¼" x 28½" (2.91 x 2.14 x .72 m).
Carnegie Museum of Art, Pittsburgh. Howard Heinz Endowment Fund, 1967.
Cubi XI, 1963. Stainless steel, 9' x 32" x 39" (2.74 x .81 x .99 m). Calvin Cafritz.
Cubi II, 1963. Stainless steel, 10'10½" x 36⅞" x 23⅜" (3.31 x .94 x .59 m).
The Collection of Candida and Rebecca Smith.
Lower right: *Aggressive Character,* 1947. Stainless steel and wrought iron,
32½ x 4 x 7½", on wood base, 1¾ x 7 x 8¼ " (4.45 x 17.78 x 20.96 cm).
The Collection of Candida and Rebecca Smith,
courtesy National Gallery of Art, Washington, D.C. All photographs by David Smith.

You know, he always used to say he was a welder,
which was completely untrue. You couldn't have met more of an artist
however far you would look, but he didn't like to stress that.
I think his creative process was his life.

—ANTHONY CARO

Cubis and related works in the 1999 exhibition, from left to right:
Cubi XXII, 1964. Stainless steel, 8' 7¾" x 6'¾" x 35" (2.66 x 1.85 x .89 m). Yale University Art Gallery, Stephen Carlton Clark, B.A. 1903, Fund.
Cubi XXVII, 1965. Stainless steel, 9'3⅜" x 7'3¾" x 34" (2.83 x 2.23 x .86 m).
Solomon R. Guggenheim Museum, New York. By exchange, 1967.
Cubi V, 1963. Stainless steel, 8' x 6'1" x 22" (2.44 x 1.85 x .56 m). Jon and Mary Shirley.
Untitled, 1964. Stainless steel, 8'1" x 5'3" x 27½" (2.46 x 1.60 x .70 m).
Collection Art Gallery of Ontario, Toronto. Purchased with the assistance of the Women's Committee Fund, 1968.
Seen through the circle of *Untitled*, 1964: *Superstructure on 4*, 1960.
Below right: *Books and Apple*, 1957. Silver, 30 x 21 x 4⅞" (76.20 x 53.34 x 12.38 cm).
Fogg Art Museum, Harvard University Art Museums. Gift of Lois Orswell. All photographs by David Smith.

In the stainless steel work, he thought of the sky, the clouds, the sun, the seasonal changes, the foliage, the reflection. The vision he had was to incorporate and work with nature.

— DAN BUDNIK

Left: *Untitled*, 1964. Stainless steel, 9'9⅝" x 5'9" x 16¾" (2.99 x 1.75 x .43 m).
Collection of The Newark Museum, Purchase 1967, The Charles W. Engelhard Foundation Fund.
Above: *Untitled (Candida)*, 1965. Stainless steel, 8'6¾" x 10' x 31¼" (2.61 x 3.05 x .79 m). The Collection of Candida and Rebecca Smith.
Photographs by Jerry L. Thompson.

Horse, 1961. Silver and gold, 13⅝ x 7¾ x 2¼" (34.61 x 19.69 x 5.72 cm).
Private collection. Photograph by Peter Stevens. Right: *Becca*, 1965.
Stainless steel, 9'5½" x 10'½" x 30" (2.88 x 3.06 x .76 m).
Lent by The Metropolitan Museum of Art. Bequest of Miss Adelaide Milton de Groot (1876–1967), by exchange, 1972 (1972.127).
Photographed in the lower field at Bolton Landing in 1965 by Dan Budnik, with *Cubi VI*, 1963, at left, and *5 Ciarcs*, 1963, at right.

Does the onlooker realize the amount of affection which goes into a work of art—
the intense affection—belligerent vitality—and total conviction?

—DAVID SMITH

Self-portrait, c. 1962.

David Smith: A Selected Chronology *compiled by* JOAN PACHNER

Titles appearing in **bold** type indicate works shown in one or more of the three years of the Storm King exhibition.

1906
Born David Roland Smith, March 9, 1906, in Decatur, Indiana

1925
SUMMER, works as a welder and riveter for Studebaker automobile factory in South Bend, Indiana, assembling steel frames for cars.

FALL, enrolls at University of Notre Dame, but drops out after two weeks when he realizes no art courses are offered. Returns to work for Studebaker, but in their Finance Department, which transfers him to Morris Plan Bank in Washington, D. C.

1926
FALL, transferred to New York City. Meets Dorothy Dehner. Following her advice, enrolls at the Art Students League, taking evening classes with Richard Lahey.

1927
FALL, studies full-time at the Art Students League (until 1931). Teachers include the American John Sloan and, most important, the Czech abstract painter Jan Matulka, former pupil of Hans Hoffman. Smith recalled: "It was from him ... that for the first time I learned of Cubism and Constructivism. Then the world kind of opened for me.... Matulka was the most notable influence on my work." Works at various part-time jobs.

DECEMBER, Marries Dorothy Dehner.

1928
Takes drawing classes with Kimon Nicholaides; continues private studies with Matulka, who encourages Smith to attach found and shaped wooden objects and other materials to painting surfaces.

1929
SUMMER, visits Bolton Landing, near Lake George in the Adirondack Mountains. Smith and Dehner buy the Old Fox Farm, later renamed Terminal Iron Works.

1930
Becomes friends with artist and theorist John Graham and meets other avant-garde painters including Stuart Davis, Jean Xceron, Arshile Gorky, and Willem de Kooning. Other friends include Edgar Levy and his wife Lucille Corcos, Adolph and Esther Gottlieb, Milton and Sally Avery.

Smith works in an abstract, Surrealist style, experiments with painting, collage, and reliefs, and is increasingly interested in combining constructed compositions with painting.

1931
OCTOBER, Smith and Dehner journey to St. Thomas, Virgin Islands.

1932
SUMMER, arrives back in New York City and goes to Bolton Landing. Makes first freestanding sculpture, a coral head painted maroon, incorporating material from the Caribbean. Photographs freestanding wood constructions in the fields.

1933
Exhibits first painting, a Virgin Islands landscape, at ACA Gallery.

FALL, begins to weld sculptures using oxyacetylene torch.

1934
Discovers the Terminal Iron Works, a metal shop on the Brooklyn Navy Pier, where he rents working space; this is his main studio until 1940.

MARCH, begins work for Temporary Emergency Relief Administration (TERA).

1935
JULY, leaves work with TERA.

OCTOBER, sails to Europe with Dehner. Visits Brussels, Paris, Greece, Crete, Naples, Malta, Russia, and London.

1936
JULY, returns to New York City.

Cited by John Graham, in *System and Dialectics of Art*, as one of the outstanding young American painters.

1937
FEBRUARY, works again for the Treasury Department surveying post office for murals and mural installation. Later joins the Sculpture Division of the Works Projects Administration (WPA).

Works on Medals for Dishonor (until 1940).

1938
Blue Construction

JANUARY, first solo exhibition at Marian Willard's East River Gallery in New York City.

1939
Head 3 (Head as Still Life)

Included in the New York World's Fair exhibition "American Art Today."

1940
SPRING, Smith and Dehner move permanently upstate to the Bolton Landing property; renames his home and studio Terminal Iron Works. Works as a machinist in Glens Falls, near Bolton Landing.

1941
Studies welding at a wartime government school in Warrensburg, New York.

1942
Electricity comes to the road just outside the farm. Smith builds new cinder-block, open-plan machine-shop studio with a concrete floor (completed 1943).

JULY (until 1944), lives in Schenectady, near Albany. Studies welding at Union College and works the graveyard shift for American Locomotive Company assembling M7 destroyer tanks and locomotives seven days a week. Joins United Steelworkers of America, Local 2054; is rated first-class armor-plate welder by army ordinance.

1944
Classic Figure III (Abstract Figure)

SUMMER, moves back to Bolton Landing; works on building new studio and home.

1945–47
Construction with Cheese Clouds (1945)
Perfidious Albion (The British Empire) of 1945
Steel Drawing I (1945)
Steel Drawing II (1945–52)
Euterpe and Terpsichore (1946)
Landscape with Strata (1946)
Personage from Stove City (1946)
Aggressive Character (1947)

Immediate postwar work is strongly symbolic in content; formal invention affected by Surrealist imagery and ideas, such as ***Perfidious Albion (The British Empire)*** of 1945. Others, like ***Personage from Stove City*** (1946), explore the relationship between painting and sculpture.

Begins to make radically new sculptures on the traditionally pictorial subject of landscape, including ***Landscape with Strata*** (1946).

JANUARY 1946, retrospective at Willard and Buchholz Galleries of fifty-four sculptures.

APRIL 1947, exhibition catalogue at Willard Gallery includes poems "The Landscape," "Spectres Are," and "Sculpture Is."

1948
First teaching position at Sarah Lawrence College, Bronxville, near New York City (until 1950).

1949
Portrait of the Eagle's Keeper (1948–49)
Royal Incubator

Completes new house at Bolton Landing.

1950–51
All Around the Square (Inside the Marble Cube) (1951)
Arc Wing (1951)
Stainless Window (1951)

APRIL 1950, receives Guggenheim Foundation Fellowship; renewed 1951. Temporarily frees Smith from teaching. Uses money to immediately buy a large stock of quality materials. The scale of his work expands dramatically and his forms become more lyrical; new artistic maturity.

Smith begins to make sustained series of works over many years; these dominate his later career. First series is the Agricolas; the series eventually includes twenty-two different sculptures, the last one made in 1959.

1952
Agricola VII
Vertical Pistol Structure

Begins Tanktotem series, eventually comprising ten sculptures made between 1953 and 1960; the last five in the series are painted (1957–60). Each Tanktotem incorporates part of prefabricated concave and convex boiler tops that Smith orders from a catalogue. He continued to work on them ten years later: "I'm still working on them and don't rule them out until the day I die – that is, as long as concave and convex are still a mystery."

Divorced from Dorothy Dehner.

1953
Untitled (c. 1953)

JANUARY, *ARTnews* votes Smith's 1952 exhibition at Willard-Kleeman Gallery one of the ten best shows of the year.

SPRING, resumes teaching as Visiting Artist at the University of Arkansas, Fayetteville. Marries Jean Freas.

1954
Egyptian Barnyard
Portrait of a Painter
Portrait of a Young Girl
The Sitting Printer (1954–55)
Untitled
First state of *The Iron Woman* (1954–58)

In the middle and late 1950s is visited by Jackson Pollock, Lee Krasner, and Willem de Kooning.

APRIL, Rebecca (Eve Athena Allen Katherine Rebecca) is born, Glens Falls, New York.

Makes *Egyptian Barnyard*, one of six silver sculptures, for Towle Silversmiths, Newburyport, Massachusetts, included in the exhibition "Sculpture in Silver from Islands in Time," circulated by the American Federation of Arts, 1955–56.

JUNE, featured in XXVII Venice Biennale exhibition, "2 Painters 3 Sculptors," organized by the Museum of Modern Art. Smith visits Europe for the first time since 1936, traveling to Venice as a delegate to UNESCO's First International Congress of Plastic Arts; also visits France.

The installation of *Agricola I* in the north, or upper, field is filmed by Ilya Bolotowsky.

AUGUST, makes *Portrait of a Painter* and *Portrait of a Young Girl.*

SEPTEMBER 1954 (TO JUNE 1955), Visiting Professor, Department of Fine Arts, Indiana University, Bloomington. Sends found stool pieces and printer's box to be sand-cast in bronze in Syracuse, New York. These parts will be welded together in Bolton Landing, summer 1955, to make *The Sitting Printer.*

1955
Untitled (c. 1955)
Forging IV
Untitled (Coat Rack)

In Bloomington, learns about forging from blacksmith Leroy Borton, who worked for a local steel fabricator; makes Forging series on his power forge (1955).

MARCH, leaves Bloomington for six weeks to be a Visiting Artist at the University of Mississippi, Oxford; returns to Bloomington in late April to complete the semester.

SUMMER at Bolton Landing.

AUGUST, Candida (Candida Kore Nicolina Rawley Helene) is born.

1956
Bones Fly
Bridge End (Egyptian)
Five Units Equal
Lunar Arcs on 1 Leg (1956–60)
Portrait of a Lady Painter (1954; 1956–57)
Skull and Tree (1956–57)
The Woman Bandit (1956–58)
Wild Plum

MARCH, solo exhibition at Willard Gallery; no works are sold. Smith soon terminates relationship with the gallery.

APRIL THROUGH JUNE, lives with his family in New York City in the apartment of his friend the painter Herman Cherry. During this time he conceives *Portrait of a Lady Painter.* Socializes with Jackson Pollock, Willem de Kooning, Franz Kline, Michael Goldberg, as well as younger artists such as Kenneth Noland.

According to Jean Freas, Smith installs *Australia* (1951) in the middle of the lower field.

The Iron Woman, exhibited in the Whitney Annual at the Whitney Museum of American Art, is damaged in transit and repaired by Smith, who alters the work's base before it is sent to the Venice Biennale for exhibition in 1958.

Makes new series of bronze plaques, including *Bones Fly, Bridge End (Egyptian), Skull and Tree,* and *Wild Plum.*

Painting steel surfaces in an Expressionist style, i.e. *Five Units Equal* (1956). Begins Sentinel series of eight tall sculptures.

1957
Bird
Books and Apple
Center Four Ovals (Chicago O)
Detroit Queen
Head
Lilypad Head
Lonesome Man
Pendulum Head (Clock Head)
Personage of May
Pilgrim
Raven IV
Study in Arcs
Tower Eight
Untitled (Rebecca with Turtle)

APRIL, writes that he has finished a bronze that "scares me it's so bad;" also working on "more sweet" "shovel head" [*Personage of May*].

Reading newly published books on Impressionist painting by Jean Leymarie and John Rewald.

SEPTEMBER, retrospective at the Museum of Modern Art is curated by Sam Hunter.

NOVEMBER, Smith feels he has cash to spend and places an order for a large shipment of stainless steel from U.S. Steel; makes preliminary drawings for *Tanktotem VII.*

1958
Untitled (1958–59)

JUNE, represents the United States at the XXIX Venice Biennale in the group show "Lipton, Rothko, Smith, and Tobey."

Begins to make spray enamel drawings on paper and canvas.

Begins to work with unpainted, burnished stainless steel, creating sculptures designed to be placed outdoors, with painterly, brilliantly reflective surfaces.

1959
Agricola XXII
Albany I
Auburn Queen
XI Books III Apples
Raven V
Sentinel V
Untitled

JANUARY, grant application to the Ford Foundation is rejected.

SUMMER, participates in the São Paulo Bienal.

SEPTEMBER AND OCTOBER, exhibits paintings and drawings at the new French and Company Gallery (directed by Clement Greenberg).

OCTOBER AND NOVEMBER, writes that he is "on a finishing bender, having finished up about 10 in the last two months."

Begins Albany series, fourteen smaller sculptures in steel; all except the last two are painted black.

1960
Egg Temple
Superstructure on 4
Tanktotem VII and *Tanktotem VIII*
Three Ovals Soar
Three Planes (1960–61)
Two sculptures, each *Untitled* (c. 1960)
Untitled (Chock Full O' Nuts) (c. 1960)

JANUARY, grant application to the Ford Foundation is rejected again.

FEBRUARY, important exhibition at the French and Company Gallery. Special issue of *Arts Magazine* devoted to Smith's work.

NOVEMBER, first West Coast solo exhibition at Everett Ellin Gallery, Los Angeles.

1961
Bridge End (1961 silver cast of 1956 piece)
Dida's Circle on a Fungus
Horse
Lunar Arc
Noland's Blues
Rebecca Circle
Untitled
Untitled (Standing Figure) (1961–62)
Cubi Woman (1961–62)

Smith's output continues to be dominated by painted steel works; gestural painting style also relates directly to contemporaneous ink drawings.

Smith also explores an increasingly planar style in the first white painted piece, *Lunar Arc.*

The fields are more densely filled with Smith's sculptures.

Divorced from Jean Freas.

SUMMER, daughters Rebecca and Candida are in Bolton Landing. Visits Helen Frankenthaler and Robert Motherwell in Provincetown, Massachusetts; also close friends with Herman Cherry, Clement Greenberg, and Kenneth Noland.

OCTOBER solo exhibition at Otto Gerson Gallery; participates in Carnegie Institute "Pittsburgh International"; refuses third prize and suggests that the $1000 award be used to purchase a work of art for the museum.

Gestural painting style also affects the surfaces of the new stainless steel Cubi series, beginning with *Cubi IX.*

1962
Three Planes (Small Version for Candida) (c. 1962)
Albany XI
Circle IV
2 Circle IV
Primo Piano II and *Primo Piano III*
Untitled
Voltri V, Voltri VIII, Voltri XVI, and *Voltri XIX*
Voltri-Bolton III and *Voltri-Bolton X*

The circle, a recurrent element in Smith's work since the late 1930s, becomes an important conceptual and formal thematic element in his late works.

MAY UNTIL JULY, travels to Italy to participate in "Fourth Festival of Two Worlds," Spoleto. Intends to continue work with stainless steel, but is offered access to five abandoned factories and six assistants. Using a combination of found objects and created shapes, makes twenty-seven Voltri sculptures during his one month stay; they are displayed outdoors on the steps of Spoleto's ancient amphitheater.

JULY, returns to Bolton Landing and begins to place completed sculptures outside in the upper field.

OCTOBER (until January 1963), creates polychrome Circles, improvisational Voltri-Boltons, and volumetric Cubis.

DECEMBER, Dan Budnik arrives at Bolton Landing to photograph Smith at work. Sculptures in process include *Primo Piano III* and the first of the Voltri-Bolton series, made using materials shipped to Bolton Landing from Italy in large quantities.

1963
Volton XIII, Volton XVI, Volton XVIII, Volton XX, VB XXI and V.B. XXII
Menand VII
Circle and Box
Oval Node
Tower I
2 Circles 2 Crows
Untitled
Cubi I, Cubi II, Cubi V, Cubi XI, Cubi XIII

MARCH, completes Voltri-Bolton series. Budnik returns to Bolton Landing.

"David Smith's Steel Goliaths," profile in *Life* magazine, April 5, features Budnik's photographs.

Continues white-painted sculptures, including *Oval Node* and *Untitled.*

SUMMER, Mark di Suvero visits Smith in Bolton Landing.

FALL, Anthony Caro visits Smith in Bolton Landing.

SEPTEMBER, makes small painted volumetric Menand series.

OCTOBER, teaches at Bennington College, Vermont, one day a week.

1964
Becca (Steel)
Construction December II
Untitled (Newark)
Untitled (Ontario)
Cubi XXII and *Cubi XXIV*

Smith asserts, "I'm going to make [my sculptures] so big that they can't ever be moved."

Creates three large, flat stainless steel open circles, his most abstract works to date.

Receives Brandeis University Creative Arts Award.

SUMMER, *Cubi I* is exhibited at "Documenta III," Kassel, Germany. Irving Sandler visits Smith in Bolton Landing.

OCTOBER, first solo exhibition at Marlborough-Gerson Gallery includes eight Cubis, two Zigs, and a group of Menands. Interview with Frank O'Hara televised on WNTD-TV: "David Smith: Welding Master of Bolton Landing."

1965
Becca (Stainless steel)
Hi Candida
Untitled (Candida)
Cubi XXVII

FEBRUARY, appointed by President Lyndon B. Johnson to the National Council on the Arts.

Actively involved in planning upcoming retrospective at Los Angeles County Museum of Art (opens in November as "David Smith: A Memorial Exhibition").

MAY, Alexander Liberman, Helen Frankenthaler, and Robert Motherwell visit Bolton Landing. Liberman's photographs are the last record of the artist and his work.

MAY 23, driving in Bennington, Vermont, his truck overturns. He dies that night. There are eighty-nine sculptures in the fields.

Lenders to the Exhibition

Art Gallery of Ontario, Toronto
The Baltimore Museum of Art
Leonard and Adele Blumberg
Irma and Norman Braman
Donald L. Bryant, Jr. Family Trust
Calvin Cafritz
Carnegie Museum of Art, Pittsburgh
Cleveland Museum of Art
The Detroit Institute of Arts
Helen Frankenthaler
Solomon R. Guggenheim Museum, New York
Harvard University Art Museums
Hirshhorn Museum and Sculpture Garden, Smithsonian Institution, Washington, D.C.
Indianapolis Museum of Art
Dr. and Mrs. Arthur E. Kahn
The Menil Collection, Houston
The Metropolitan Museum of Art, New York
Museo de Arte Contemporáneo Internacional Rufino Tamayo, México
Museum of American Art of the Pennsylvania Academy of the Fine Arts, Philadelphia
Raymond D. Nasher, Dallas, Texas
The Newark Museum
Mr. and Mrs. David N. Pincus
The John B. Putnam, Jr. Memorial Collection, Princeton University
Sheldon Memorial Art Gallery and Sculpture Garden, University of Nebraska, Lincoln
Jon and Mary Shirley
The Collection of Candida and Rebecca Smith
Mr. and Mrs. Harold P. Starr
The State of New York Governor Nelson A. Rockefeller Empire State Plaza State Art Collection, Albany, New York
Jerome and Ellen Stern
Bagley and Virginia Wright
Yale University Art Gallery, New Haven, Connecticut
Anonymous lenders

Benefactors

TO THE EXHIBITION

Major funding has been provided by the Ralph E. Ogden Foundation, Inc.

Additional contributions have been received from

Glen Eagles Foundation
Ralph E. Ogden Foundation, Inc.
Mr. and Mrs. Ernst Ohnell
The Howard Phipps Foundation
The Frederick W. Richmond Foundation

Anonymous benefactors

TO THE CATALOGUE

Major funding has been provided by the Ralph E. Ogden Foundation, Inc., and Mr. and Mrs. James H. Ottaway, Jr.

Additional contributions have been received from

The Richard and Eslyn Bassuk Foundation, Inc.
Dedalus Foundation, Inc.
Doris and Donald Fisher
Mary W. Harriman Foundation
Vera G. List
Ralph E. Ogden Foundation, Inc.
Mr. and Mrs. Ernst Ohnell
Mr. and Mrs. James H. Ottaway, Jr.
Ruth Turner
Bagley and Virginia Wright